DONCASTER TO HULL
and Gilberdyke to Selby

Vic Mitchell & Keith Smith

Middleton Press

Front cover: Power car no. 43316 leads an afternoon Edinburgh-Kings Cross express into Doncaster station on the afternoon of 22nd February 2011. The train carries the former National Express livery but with 'East Coast' branding since National Express had withdrawn from the franchise in 2009. (P.D.Shannon)

Back cover picture: Waiting under the splendid roof at Hull Paragon on 9th March 2015 is no. 170309 plus Pacer no. 142052. (Colour-Rail.com)

Back cover map: The Railway Clearing House map of 1947.

ACKNOWLEDGEMENTS

We are very grateful for the assistance received from many of those mentioned in the credits, also from A.J.Castledine, G.Gartside, J.Hinson (Signalling Record Society), C.M.Howard, N.Langridge, B.Lewis, A.Neale, D.Salter, M.Stewart, J.Suter, T.Walsh and, in particular, our always supportive families.

Published November 2020

ISBN 978 1 910356 49 4

© Middleton Press Ltd, 2020

Picture enhancing & Cover Deborah Esher
Typesetting & Design Cassandra Morgan

Published by
    Middleton Press
    Easebourne Lane
    Midhurst
    West Sussex
    GU29 9AZ
Tel: 01730 813169
Email: info@middletonpress.co.uk
www.middletonpress.co.uk

Printed and bound by CPI Group (UK) Ltd, Croydon, CR0 4YY

CONTENTS

1. Doncaster to Hull   1-98
2. Gilberdyke to Selby   99-120

INDEX

13	Barnby Dun	44	Gilberdyke	12	Kirk Sandall
47	Broomfleet	27	Goole	65	Melton Halt
53	Brough	15	Hatfield & Stainforth	36	Saltmarshe
52	Crabley Creek	108	Hemingbrough	117	Selby
1	Doncaster	72	Hessle	43	Staddlethorpe
99	Eastrington	103	Howden	22	Thorne North
70	Ferriby	91	Hull	106	Wressle

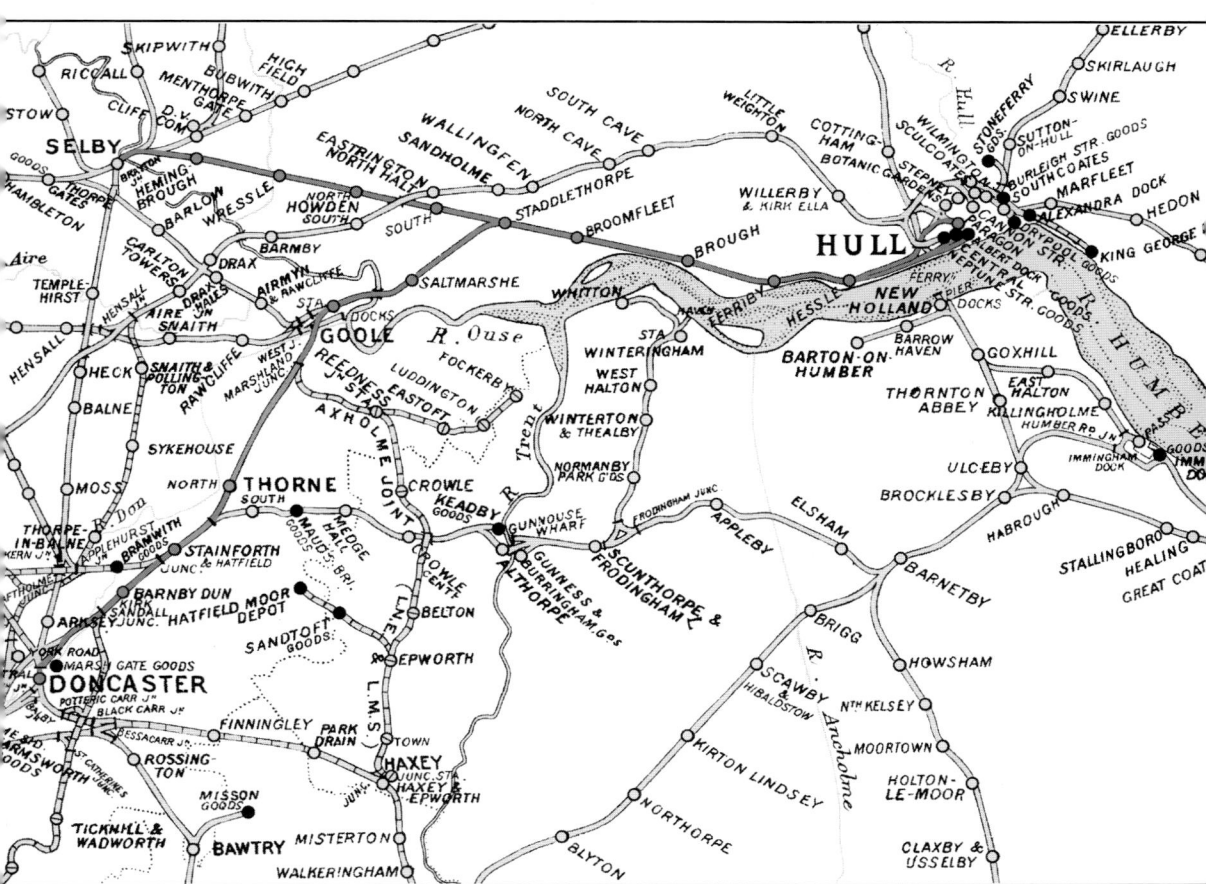

I. The Railway Clearing House diagram of 1947 has the route of this album in dark grey. The maps herein are to the scale of 25ins to 1 mile, with north at the top, unless otherwise indicated.

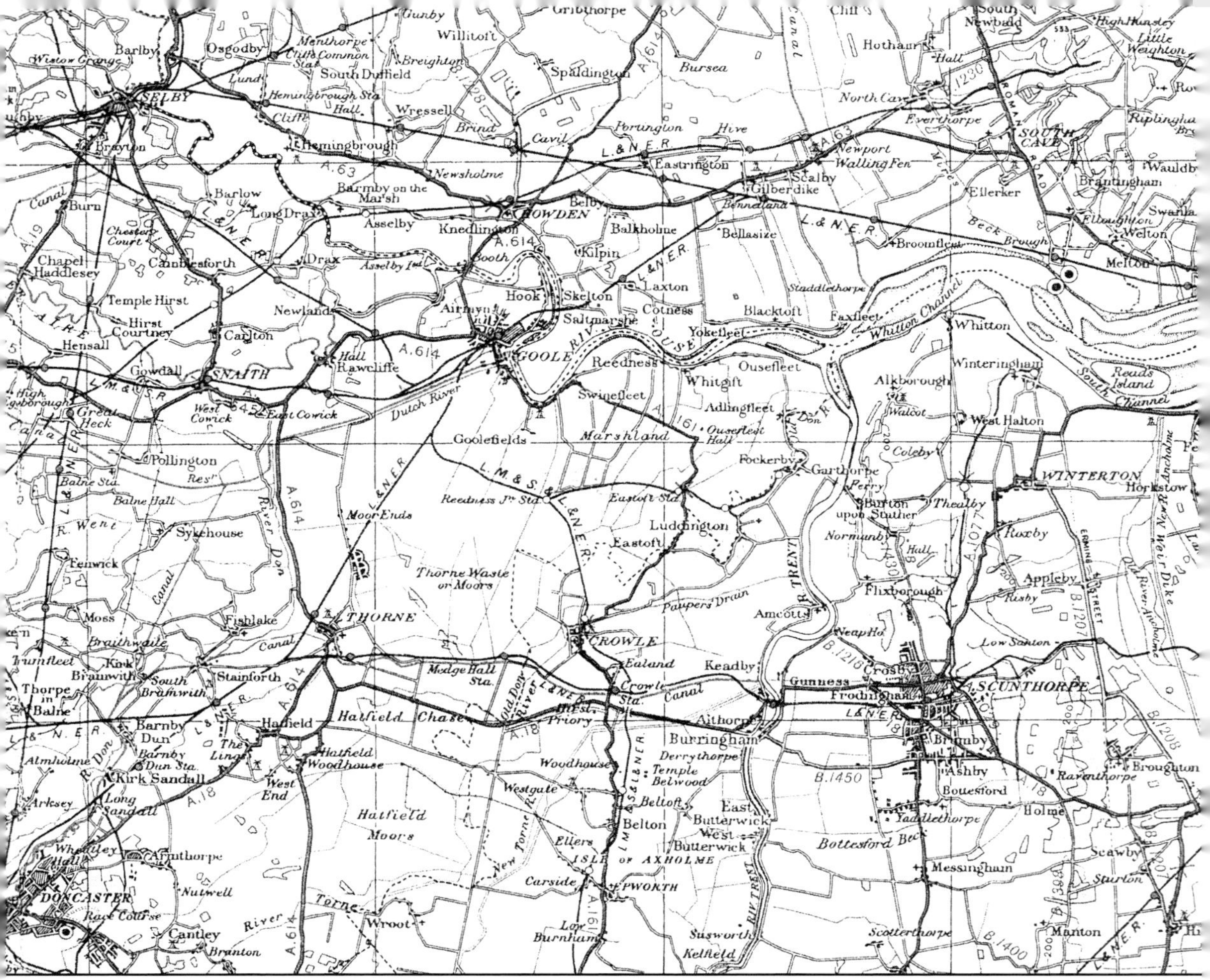

GEOGRAPHICAL SETTING

This journey is over unusually level ground, which has a surface of sandstone mainly. Its lower strata contain many beds of coal; the mines working them will soon be seen.

The route east of Broomfleet runs over a number of different outcrops, but from Ferriby into Hull the terrain is mostly on chalk.

Water traverses or is close to the entire system. Doncaster has the River Don (also called the River Dun in some stretches) and the River Cheswold adjacent, with a number of man-made cuts and canals serving the community. North of Thorne, the Don and the adjacent New Junction Canal flow into the Dutch River, which was created by a Dutch engineer.

Selby and Goole both had the benefit of the River Ouse becoming navigable. It joins the River Humber, which flows into the North Sea and has conveyed much commercial traffic to and from the countries bordering that sea.

It does appear to many that the line between Selby and Brough (around 18 miles long) is the longest stretch of straight track in the country.

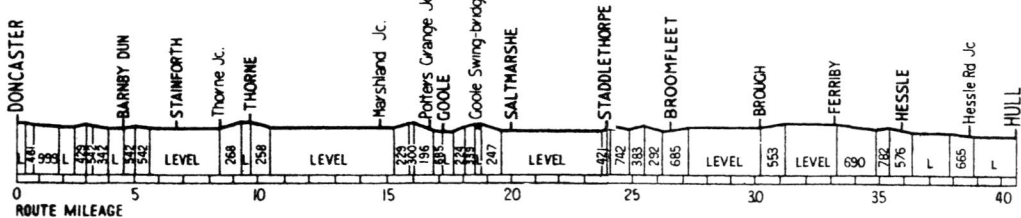

← II. We start in the lower left corner, and run northeast to 'Gilberdike'. BR used 'Gilberdyke' from 1974. We then go east to Ferriby, on the way to Hull. Part 2 of this album starts at the former and goes west, straight to Selby. This 1947 issue is scaled at ¼ in to 1 mile.

HISTORICAL BACKGROUND

The Leeds & Selby Railway was one of the first in the UK and was promoted mainly to help move wool from Europe to Leeds. Initially, most of it was transferred at Hull into the small boats of the day and they used the Humber and the River Ouse for the final part of the journey. The line was opened to the public on 22nd September 1834.

Doncaster received the Great Northern Railway from the north in 1848 and its extension southwards in 1849. Also that year was the completion of the South Yorkshire, Doncaster & Goole line from the west. In the next year, its name became the South Yorkshire & River Dun Navigation Railway. It opened a line from Doncaster to Thorne on 11th December 1855 using the formation of a canal, and extended east through Scunthorpe to Barnetby by the Trent, Ancholme & Grimsby Railway on 1st October 1866. Here it joined the 1848 route of the Manchester, Sheffield and Lincolnshire Railway. This was renamed the Great Central Railway in 1897, the TA&GR having joined the MS&LR in 1882. The GCR became a large part of the London & North Eastern Railway in the grouping of 1923.

The line northeast from Doncaster to Thorne was realigned on a straighter route on 1st October 1866, and the North Eastern Railway opened from Thorne Junction via Goole to Staddlethorpe on 2nd August 1869.

The Hull & Selby Railway arrived from the west through Brough in 1840 and from the north, via Beverley, in 1846. The York & North Midland Railway opened the line into Hull Paragon in 1848. These lines became part of the North Eastern Railway in 1872 and this gained the prefix 'London &' in 1923.

The Hull & Holderness Railway opened its route from Hull to Withernsea on 27th June 1854. However, its trains started from Victoria Dock in Hull until 1st July 1864. The H&HR began services on its branch to Hornsea on 28th March 1864. It was worked by the NER from the outset, but trains from Hornsea terminated at Wilmington until 1st July 1864.

The LNER formed part of the North Eastern Region of British Railways upon nationalisation in 1948 and this included the lines herein. The area became part of the Eastern Region in 1967. Goods service withdrawals are noted in the captions.

Privatisation

On the first part of the route, from Doncaster to Gilberdyke, services were initially operated by Regional Railways North East from 2nd March 1997, which was re-branded as Northern Spirit in May 1998 and became Arriva Trains Northern on 27th April 2001. This, in part, formed a new Northern franchise on 12th December 2004, to be replaced by another new Northern franchise on 1st April 2016 and another on 1st March 2020, when the nationalised Northern Trains took over.

Services between Selby, Gilberdyke and Hull were operated as above until 1st February 2004, when some services were transferred to a new TransPennine Express (TPE) franchise, operated by First-Keolis. This was replaced by another TransPennine Express franchise on 1st April 2016, run by First. Services on this route were also operated by LNER and Hull Trains.

PASSENGER SERVICES

Bradshaw's 1847 issue showed Selby to Hull to have seven weekday trains, two on Sundays and one extra on Tuesdays for a nearby market day. The 1865 issue showed that journey having 9, 2 and 0, respectively. Right are summaries from selected years.

	Slow	Fast	Sundays
1890	3	4	3
1922	4	8	0
1950	6	10	8
1980	15	6	9

The Doncaster to Gilberdyke route has two Northern services per hour. The Selby to Gilberdyke route sees an hourly TPE service from Manchester Piccadilly, hourly Northern services from York and Leeds and services from London Kings Cross, operated by Hull Trains and LNER at roughly two-hourly intervals. All services continue beyond Gilberdyke to Hull, with limited extensions to Beverley.

→ August 1893

YORK and LEEDS to GASCOIGNE WOOD, SELBY, &c. — Week Days

(Timetable with Fares columns: Single 1cl/3cl, Return 1cl/3cl; stations including York, Copmanthorpe, Bolton Percy, Ulleskelf, Church Fenton, Sherburn, Milford arr., L'pool (Exch.), M'chester (Vic.), London (St. Pan.), Sheffield, Normanton, Milford dep., Gascoigne Wood arr., L'pool (Lime St.), M'chester (Ex.), Leeds New Stn / Marsh Ln., Cross Gates, Garforth, Micklefield, South Milford, Gascoigne Wood arr., Gascoigne Wd. dp., Milford arr., Gascoigne Wood dep., Hambleton, Selby arr., London (King's C.), York, Selby dep., Hemingbrough, Wressle, Howden, Eastrington, Staddlethorpe, Brough, Ferriby, Hessle, Hull — with multiple mrn/aft departure columns and notes "Through to Bridlington", "Saturdays only", "Tuesdays only", "Fridays only", "For Notes and Continuation of Trains, see opposite page.")

↓ 1841

HULL AND SELBY

STATIONS.	Up Trains. Mail					Sundays. Mail	Mail	STATIONS.	Down Trains. Mail					Sundays. Mail	Mail
	a.m.	a.m.	p.m.	p.m.	p.m.	a.m.	p.m.	Departure fr.	p.m.	a.m.	a.m.	a.m.	a.m.	p.m.	p.m.
Departure from								London	9 0	..	..	6 0	9 15	..	..
Hull........	6 0	8 9	11 0	2 0	5 0	8 9	5 0	Birmingham	12 40	..	..	6 45	10 45	12 40	..
Hessle.......	6 16	8 25	11 17	2 16	5 16	8 24	5 15	Derby.....	3 19	..	..	9 30	12 45	3 19	7 0
Ferriby......	6 24	8 33	11 26	2 24	5 24	8 31	5 22	Sheffield.....	..	6 0	..	10 45	1 50	4 30	8 45
Brough......	6 32	8 41	11 35	2 32	5 32	8 38	5 30	Swinton......	..	6 28	..	11 33	..	5 14	9 25
Staddlethorpe	6 48	..	..	2 48	..	6 48	5 45	Oakenshaw	5 35	7 15	..	12 15	..	5 48	5 35 10 12
Eastrington...	6 56	..	..	2 56	..	6 56	5 52								
Howden.....	7 5	9 10	12 5	3 5	6 0	7 5	9 10	6 1	Manchester	..	..	7 0	11 30	1 10	4 45	11 30
Cliff........	7 21	..	..	3 21	..	7 21	6 16	Sowerby Brid	..	6 20	8 30	12 50	2 52	5 0	12 50
Selby.......	7 30	9 34	12 30	3 30	6 25	7 30	9 34	6 25	Wakefield	..	7 18	9 22	1 38	3 49	6 53	1 38
Leeds (arrival)	8 50	10 34	1 50	4 50	7 45	8 45	10 38	7 25	Normanton	..	7 30	9 39	1 55	4	7 10	1 55
York (ditto)	8 50	10 34	..	4 50	..	8 45	7 25								
Darlington...	11 45	1 45	..	7 0	..	..	..	Darlington	..	..	6 15	..	12 45	3 30	..
Normanton..	9	10 41	1 40	4 25	7 40	..	10 41	7 40	York......	..	..	7 25	9 30	..	4 0	7 15	6 11
Wakefield ..	9 20	10 56	1 56	4 40	7 55	..	10 56	7 55	Leeds.....	6 11	7 25	9 30	..	4 0	7 15	6 11	1 35
Manchester..	11 25	1 1	4 40	6 45	..	1 1	10 0	Selby.....	7 11	8 45	10 50	2 50	5 20	8 35	7 11	2 50
Swinton......	10 46	..	..	5 48	..	..	..	Cliff....	..	8 53	10 58	..	5 28	8 43	7 19	2 58
Sheffield (arrival)	11 15	..	..	6 30	8 45	..	8 45	Howden	7 33	9	9 11 14	3 13	5 44	8 59	7 34	3 13
Derby.......	12 45	..	4 15	8 30	10	..	10 9	Eastrington	..	9 17	11 22	..	5 52	9	7 41	3 21
Nottingham (arrl.)	2 15	..	5 15	9 35	..	..	..	Staddlethorp	..	9 25	11 30	..	6 0	9 15	7 48	3 29
Leicester (arrival)	2 40	..	6 0	10 10	12 0	..	12 0	Brough.....	8 3	9 41	11 46	3 43	6 16	9 31	8 3	3 43
Birmingham..	4 30	..	6 45	..	1 0	..	1 0	Ferriby....	8 11	9 49	11 54	3 51	6 24	9 39	8 10	3 51
London......	7 45	..	11 15	..	5 0	..	5 30	Hessle.....	8 20	9 58	12 3	4 0	6 33	9 48	8 29	4 0
								Hull.....	8 36	10 15	12 20	4 15	6 50	10 5	8 36	4 15

☞ There is a train from London on Sundays at 8 a.m which arrives in Hull about 10 5 p.m.

Fares — 1st class 2d class
Hull to Selby 5s 0d 3s 6d 2s 6d
„ York 8 6 6 0 4 6
„ Leeds .. 10 0 7 6 5 6

Hull to Sheffield 16s 6d 12s 0d —
„ Normanton 9 6 7 0 5 0
„ Derby £1 5 0 17 6 —

Hull to Birmingham £1 15 0 £1 4 6
„ London.... 2 19 0 2 6 6
„ Manchester 1 3 0 0 15 6

→ February 1890

HULL, GOOLE, THORNE, and DONCASTER.—N. E.   * Stainforth & Hatfield

(Fares 1cl/2cl/3cl; stations Hull (Par. Sta.), Hessle, Ferriby, Brough, Staddlethorpe, Saltmarshe, Goole 331, Thorne, Stainfr'th 326, Barnby Dun (290), Doncaster 156, 327, 157 London (K'g's C); and reverse: 154 London (K.C.), Doncaster dep., Barnby Dun, Stainfrth & Hatfield, Thorne, Goole 331, Saltmarshe, Staddlethorpe, Brough [299], Ferriby, Hessle [& above], Hull 324, 328)

a Stops if required to take up.   **b** Stops if required to set down.   **c** Stops if required to take up for L. & Y. Stas. beyond Goole.   **d** Stop if required to take up for Doncaster & beyond.   **e** Stops on Weds. if required to take up for Goole.   **f** Stops on Weds. if required to set down.   **g** Stops at Broomfleet at 8 17 mrn. on Tuesdays to take up for Hull.   **h** Stop if required to set down from beyond Doncaster, and from L. & Y. Stas. beyond Goole.   **i** Stops if required to set down through ticket holders from beyond Doncaster, & to set down from Goole for Selby & beyond.   **k** Stops on Saturdays, if required, to set down from Goole.   **l** Stop if required to take up for Goole and beyond.   **o** Stops on Mondays; and if required, to set down from Goole.   **p** Stops on Wednesdays to set down from Goole.   **q** Stops if required to set down from the Hornsea, Withernsea, and Scarboro' Branches.   **r** Stops when required to take up for beyond Beverley.

HOWDEN, BROUGH, and HULL.—North Eastern.

Down—Contd. **Week Days**—Continued. | **Sundays.**

NOTES.

a Stops on Saturdays when required to set down from Selby and Market Weighton Branch.
b From London Road Station.
c Stop when required to set down from Leeds, Normanton, Doncaster, and beyond, and to take up for Hull.
d Stop to set down from Swinton and Knottingley Line, Leeds, Normanton, York, and beyond, on informing the Guard at Milford.
e Leaves at 2 55 mrn. on Mondays.
f Stops when required to set down from Leeds and beyond.
g Stops to set down from Sheffield and South thereof, from Leeds, York, and Stations to Riccall, and from the G.N. and L.& Y. Lines.
h Stop if required to set down.
i Stops to set down from the Swinton and Knottingly Line, Doncaster, Normanton, Leeds, York, and beyond, on informing the Guard at Selby.
k Via Normanton.
l Passengers for Milford change at Gascoigne Wood.
m Stops when required to set down from beyond Selby for Goole and Thorne.
o Except Monday morning.
p Leaves King's Cross at 8 30 aft. on Sundays.
q Except Sunday night.
v Saturday night from London (St. Pancras).
* Station Road; ¼ mile from M.S. & L. Station.

← August 1893 *(cont.)*

↓ June 1922

↙ *(bottom)* August 2018

HULL, STADDLETHORPE, GOOLE, THORNE, and DONCASTER.—North Eastern.

NOTES.

A Leaves Riverside Quay at 8 45 mrn. on Tuesdays and Saturdays commencing June 27th in connection with Zeebrugge Steamer.
B Arrives Manchester (London Road) at 3 5 mrn. on Sundays.
d Continental Boat Train; arrives Riverside Quay at 5 28 aft. on Wednesdays and Saturdays commencing June 24th in connection with Steamer to Zeebrugge.
e Except Saturdays.
F Afternoon time.
f Stops when required to take up.
g Leaves Liverpool (Ex.) at 4 35 aft. on Saturdays.
h Liverpool (Lime St.). Passengers change trains from Victoria to Exchange stations at Manchester.
h Stop when required to set down.
k Thro' Express from Sheffield, see p. 702.
p Sets down when required from beyond Doncaster.
P Through Trains to and from Sheffield, see pages 709 and 702.

q Stops when required to take up for Goole and beyond.
r Stops when required to take up for Wakefield or beyond.
s Saturdays only.
S Stops on Saturdays when required to set down.
t Stops when required to set down from Manchester or beyond.
u Stops on Tuesdays and Wednesdays when required.
V Saturday Night.
W Stops at 9 6 aft. on Fris. and Sats.
x Leaves Manchester (London Road) at 11 mrn. on Saturdays.
X Through Carriage to and from London (King's Cross) and Hull.
Y Stops on Wednesdays when required.
* Arrives at 4 35 mrn. on Sundays.
Z Sets down if required from London (King's Cross).

¶ Paragon Station; nearly 1 mile to H. & B. (Cannon Street) Station.

For other Trains BETWEEN / PAGE
Hull and Brough 768
Hull and Staddlethorpe 768

SELBY, WISTOW, and CAWOOD.—(One class only).—North Eastern.

---

181 — LONDON - HULL — All trains HT

km			Ⓐ	Ⓐ	Ⓐ	Ⓐ	Ⓐ	Ⓐ	Ⓐ	Ⓐ		⑥	⑥	⑥	⑥	⑥		⑦	⑦	⑦	⑦	⑦	⑦
0	London Kings Cross	180 d.	Ⓐ 0726	0948	1148	1348	1548	1718	1848	2030		⑥ 0726	0948	1146	…	…		⑦ 1048	1248	1448	1722	1747	1950
170	Grantham	180 d.	0827	1050	1250	1450	1649	1829	1953	2130		0827	1049	1249	…	1550	1829	1849	2052	1147	1347	1548	1825	1852	2051
223	Retford	180 d.	0852	1111	1311	1513	1711		2015	2152		0852	1111	1311	…	1611		1911	2114	1208	1408	1610		1913	2113
251	Doncaster	180 a.	0905	1125	1325	1527	1725	1909	2028	2205		0905	1124	1324	…	1625	1904	1924	2127	1226	1423	1627	1903	1927	2127
280	Selby	a.	0926	1140	1343	1543	1743	1926	2045	2225		0926	1140	1341	…	1641	1925	1941	2144	1244	1439	1645	1922	1945	2143
330	Hull	a.	1006	1218	1417	1618	1818	2005	2122	2304		1007	1218	1416	…	1725	2003	2018	2220	1322	1518	1722	2000	2020	2218
330	Hull	177 d.	…	…	…	…	…		2131									2028						2028	
343	Beverley	177 a.	…	…	…	…	…		2144									2041						2041	

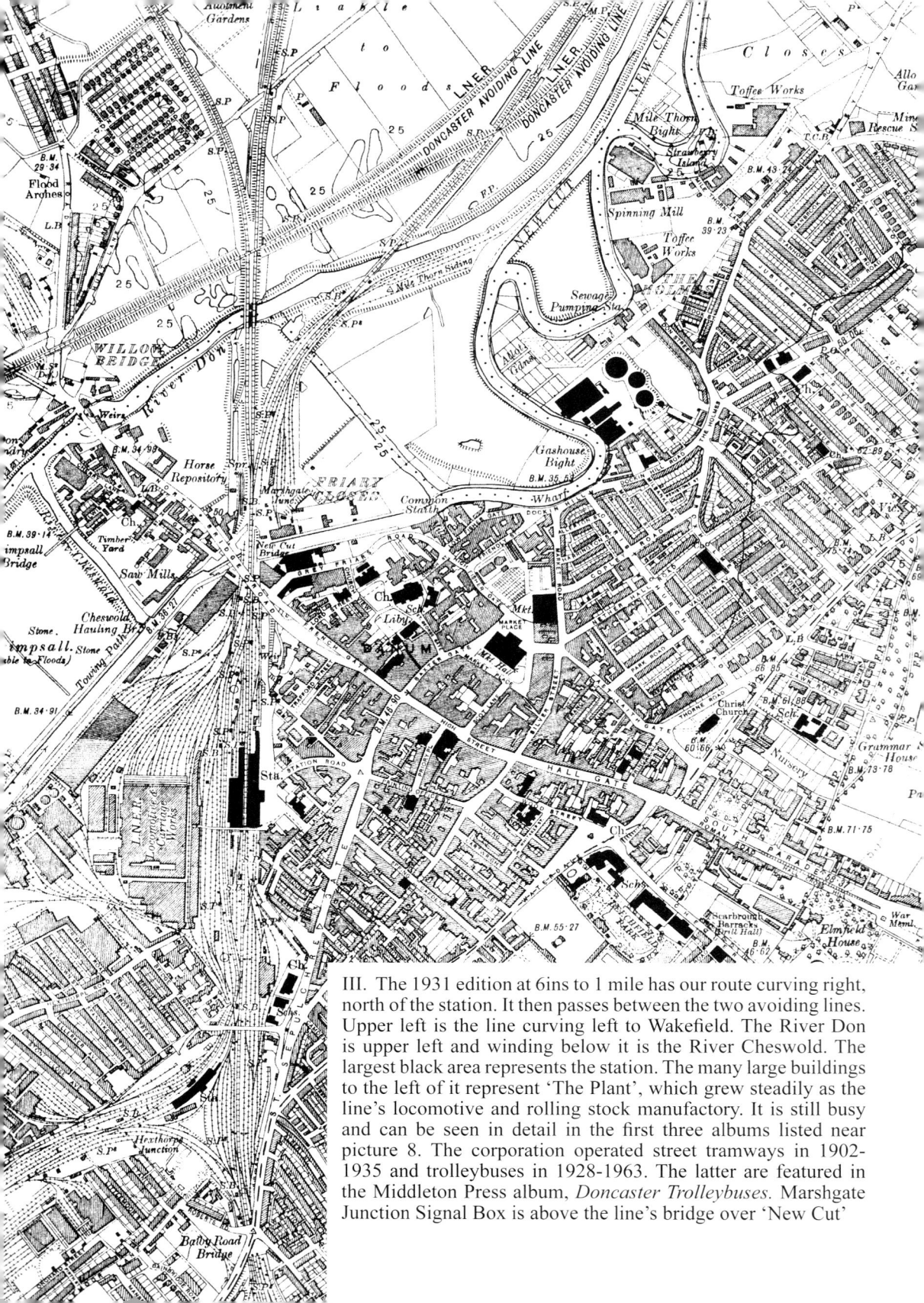

III. The 1931 edition at 6ins to 1 mile has our route curving right, north of the station. It then passes between the two avoiding lines. Upper left is the line curving left to Wakefield. The River Don is upper left and winding below it is the River Cheswold. The largest black area represents the station. The many large buildings to the left of it represent 'The Plant', which grew steadily as the line's locomotive and rolling stock manufactory. It is still busy and can be seen in detail in the first three albums listed near picture 8. The corporation operated street tramways in 1902-1935 and trolleybuses in 1928-1963. The latter are featured in the Middleton Press album, *Doncaster Trolleybuses*. Marshgate Junction Signal Box is above the line's bridge over 'New Cut'

1. Doncaster to Hull
DONCASTER

1. This postcard was sent in 1906. The details in the board are below. (Stations UK)

```
GREAT NORTHERN RAILWAY
BOOKING OFFICE FOR
LONDON - SOUTH AND WEST OF ENGLAND
NOTTINGHAM - EREWASH VALLEY - ILKESTON - DERBY
BURTON - LEICESTER - MELTON MOWBRAY - MARKET HARBORO
NORTHAMPTON - PETERBORO AND GREAT EASTERN
```

2. Working a through train is class J11 0-6-0 no. 5954. These were built in 1901-10 and this one is seen between 1923 and August 1946, when it was renumbered 4452. The canopies over the tracks were removed in around 1950. (R.Humm coll.)

3. Running through with an express to Kings Cross on 2nd July 1950 is class A4 4-6-2 no. 60029 *Woodcock*. These streamliners were introduced by the LNER in 1935. (R.G.Nelson/T.Walsh)

4. The station was spanned by two footbridges. Devoid of roofing and glazing, this footbridge was used by staff working in The Plant. Passengers still use a subway. The GNR selected Doncaster as the site for the company's locomotive, carriage and wagon works in 1851, because of its proximity to extensive coalfields and iron-founding centres. Repair shops had been established by 1853, and the first Doncaster-built loco appeared in 1867. It is 26th May 1979 and heading a Hull to Kings Cross express is no. 55022 *Royal Scots Grey*. This Co-Co type was built at the English Electric Vulcan Foundry from 1961 and the maximum speed was 100mph. (T.Heavyside)

5. The suffix CENTRAL was used in 1923-51. A view on 11th March 1982 from platform 4 reveals the complexity of the new station with its multiple chimney stacks. Parcel traffic on passenger trains would not last much longer. (D.A.Thompson/Middleton Press coll.)

6. We now have two pictures from 23rd June 1999. This is a northward view from the north of platform 4, the down slow. Single car diesel no. 153304 is setting off from platform 1, the up passenger loop, with the 10.31 to Goole. It has passed a bogie van, used as a store, at the end of the dock siding, behind which the multi-storey station car park is being built. The station was built in 1849 replacing a temporary structure constructed a year earlier. It was rebuilt in its present form in 1938-40. (A.C.Hartless)

7. Another northward view from the south end of platform 8 shows the down passenger loop. No. 156484 has arrived with the 09.43 Sheffield to Hull. The loco works footbridge dominates the area. Redundant class 141 DMUs are lined up in the works yard. (A.C.Hartless)

8. Privatisation had begun around 1995 and Hull Trains were the first to operate Open Access, starting on 23rd September 2000. Here is their first train, departing on 17th July 2014, with Adelante no. 180109 running from Hull to Kings Cross. In May 2015, construction commenced on a new platform 0 to the northeast of the station, adjacent to the Frenchgate Centre on the site of the former cattle dock. It is joined to the rest of the station via a fully accessible overbridge. (J.Whitehouse)

> **Other views are in our** *Newark to Doncaster, Lincoln to Doncaster, Mansfield to Doncaster* **and** *Scunthorpe to Doncaster* **albums. These include the locomotive works and engine sheds.** *Doncaster Trolleybuses* **has many local views.**

NORTH OF DONCASTER

Marshgate Junction

9.   This junction is ½ mile north of the station and in the background is the bridge carrying the Doncaster Avoiding Line. Hauling a long mixed freight train is class K3 2-6-0 no. 227 in LNER days. The signal box was opened in 1868 and had 28 levers when it closed on 20th February 1949. (R.Humm coll.)

Bentley Junction

10. Seen on 29th May 1974, the box controlled the triangular junction with the branch to Bentley Colliery. This box had 36 levers and was worked from 1909 to 1980. There were 1000 men in the colliery by 1910, but there was also much methane to risk their lives. (N.D.Mundy)

11. This bridge is over the River Don Navigation before reaching Kirk Sandall Junction. It is seen on 18th September 1954, whilst under repair. Passing over it is class J6 0-6-0 no. 64255. (Colour-Rail.com)

KIRK SANDALL

12. It is 24th July 2011 and we witness no. 158853 working a Scunthorpe to Doncaster service. It is about to pass under Clay Lane bridge, with the line to Tickhill & Wadworth and beyond on the right. Its first siding served Barnby Dun Rockware Glass Company's siding. Near the bridge is the platform, which opened on 13th May 1991. The Junction Box had 48 levers and was used from 1916 to 17th February 1980. (A.J.Booth)

> Our *Scunthorpe to Doncaster* album contains a closer view (picture 49), plus stations and collieries north from Hatfield Main.

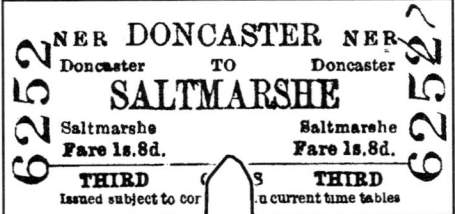

BARNBY DUN

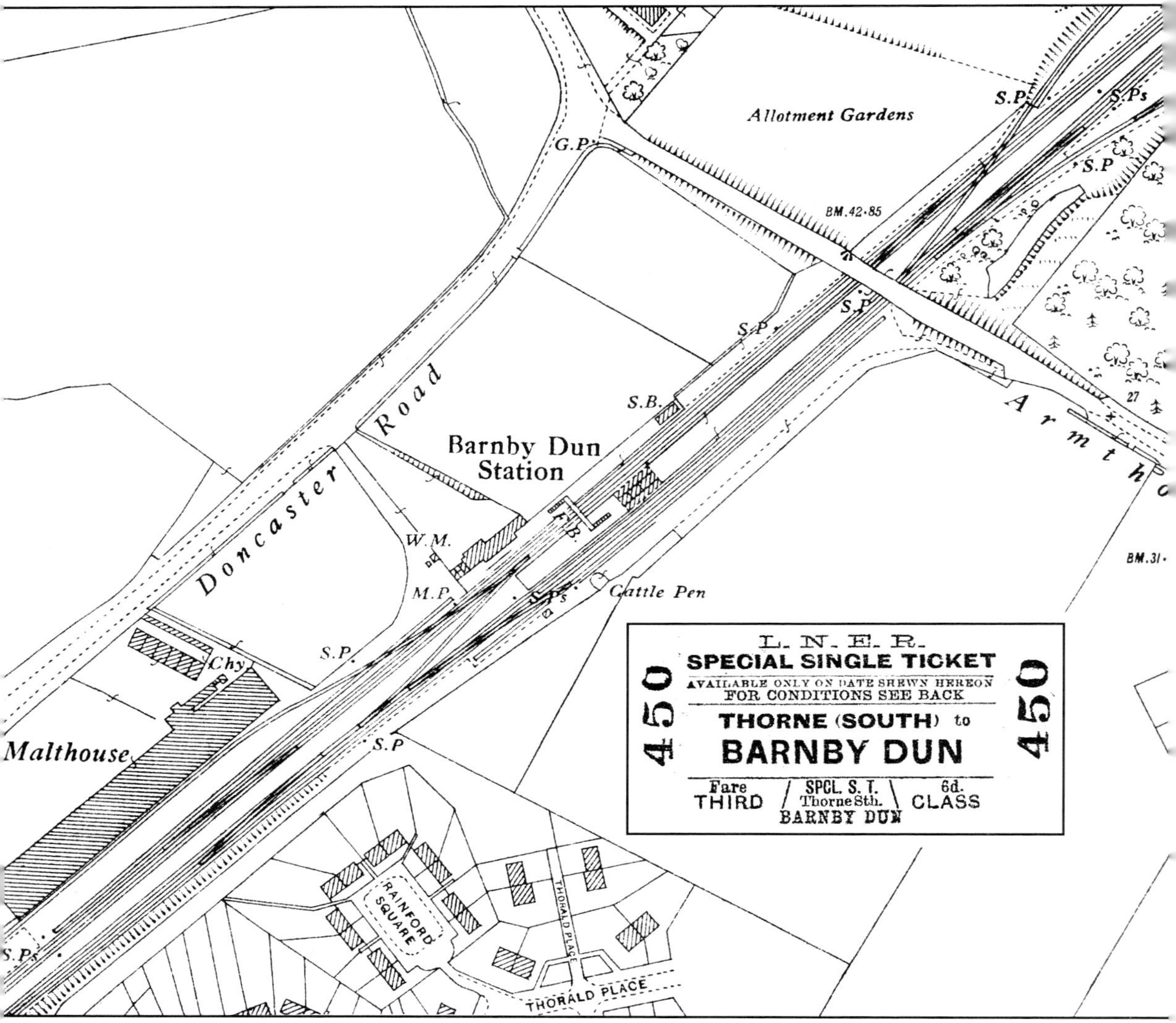

IV. The 1930 edition is shown at 25ins to 1 mile. The village had a population of 577 in 1901 and its centre was ½ mile north of the station. The first station of this name was over a mile north of the community on another route, in 1856-66. The one shown here opened with the line in 1866. The box shown (S.B.) had 95 levers from 1940, but only 77 from then until 1972 when a panel came into use.

13. This style of crossing was employed widely upon the opening of stations and it was used for passengers, staff and luggage, plus milk churns frequently. The quadrupling of the track began in 1913. (J.Alsop coll.)

14. Closure to passengers came on 4th September 1967, the goods yard having shut on 5th April 1965. Seen on 26th May 1975, the remaining buildings were demolished in 2008. A 62-lever signal box was worked from 1918 until about 1934 at Cuckoo Lane. (N.D.Mundy)

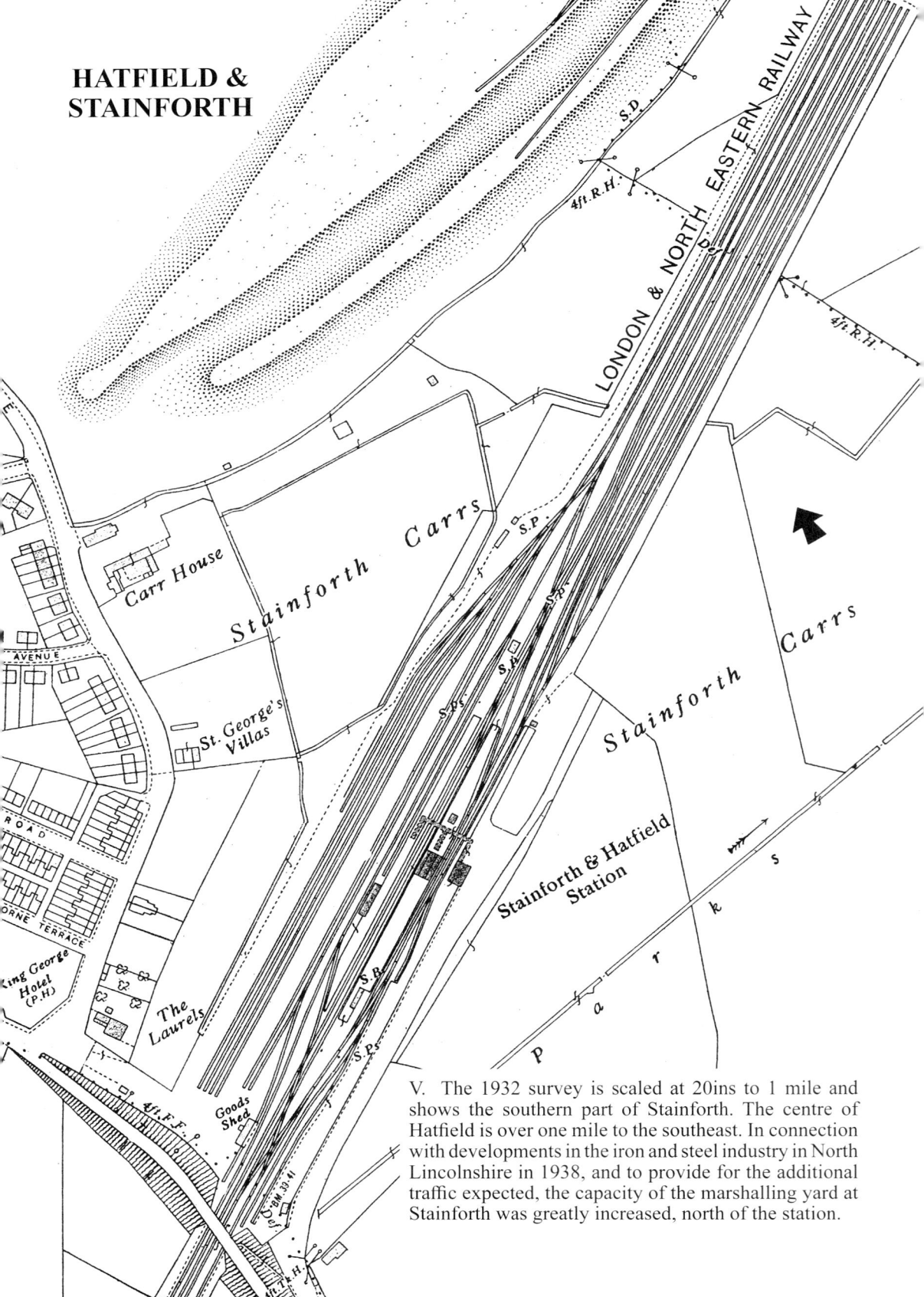

V. The 1932 survey is scaled at 20ins to 1 mile and shows the southern part of Stainforth. The centre of Hatfield is over one mile to the southeast. In connection with developments in the iron and steel industry in North Lincolnshire in 1938, and to provide for the additional traffic expected, the capacity of the marshalling yard at Stainforth was greatly increased, north of the station.

15. The initial station on the canal formation was simply Stainforth. This location dates from 1st October 1866 when the station was called Stainforth & Hatfield. The name was reversed on 28th September 1992. The wagon lettering suggests that this northward view from the road bridge is pre-1923. (J.Alsop coll.)

16. Built in 1919, 2-8-0 no. 63728 now has many rusty areas. It was rebuilt as a class O4/8 in 1956 and weighed around 73 tons. The view is from 22nd September 1962. (Colour-Rail.com)

M. S. & L. R.
Issued subject to the printed conditions
and regulations of the Company
Available on date of issue only
STAINFORTH
TO
WATH
THIRD CLASS
Stainforth
Wath
Stainforth
Wath
FARE 1/4
3804

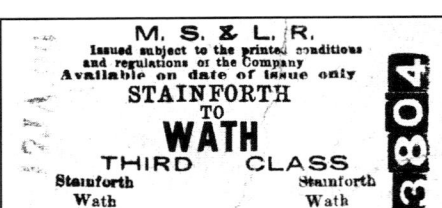

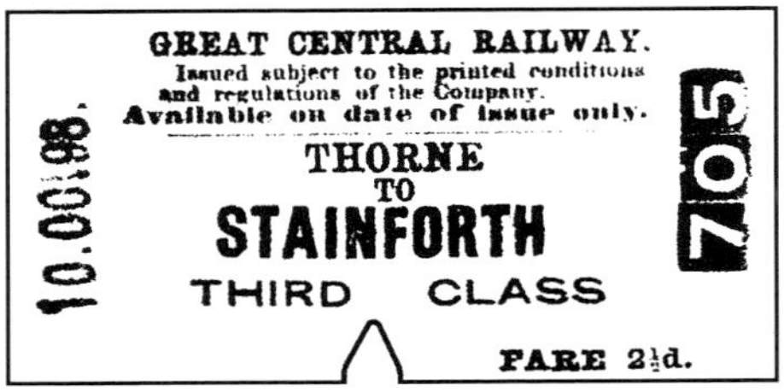
GREAT CENTRAL RAILWAY.
Issued subject to the printed conditions
and regulations of the Company.
Available on date of issue only.
THORNE
TO
STAINFORTH
THIRD CLASS
FARE 2½d.
705

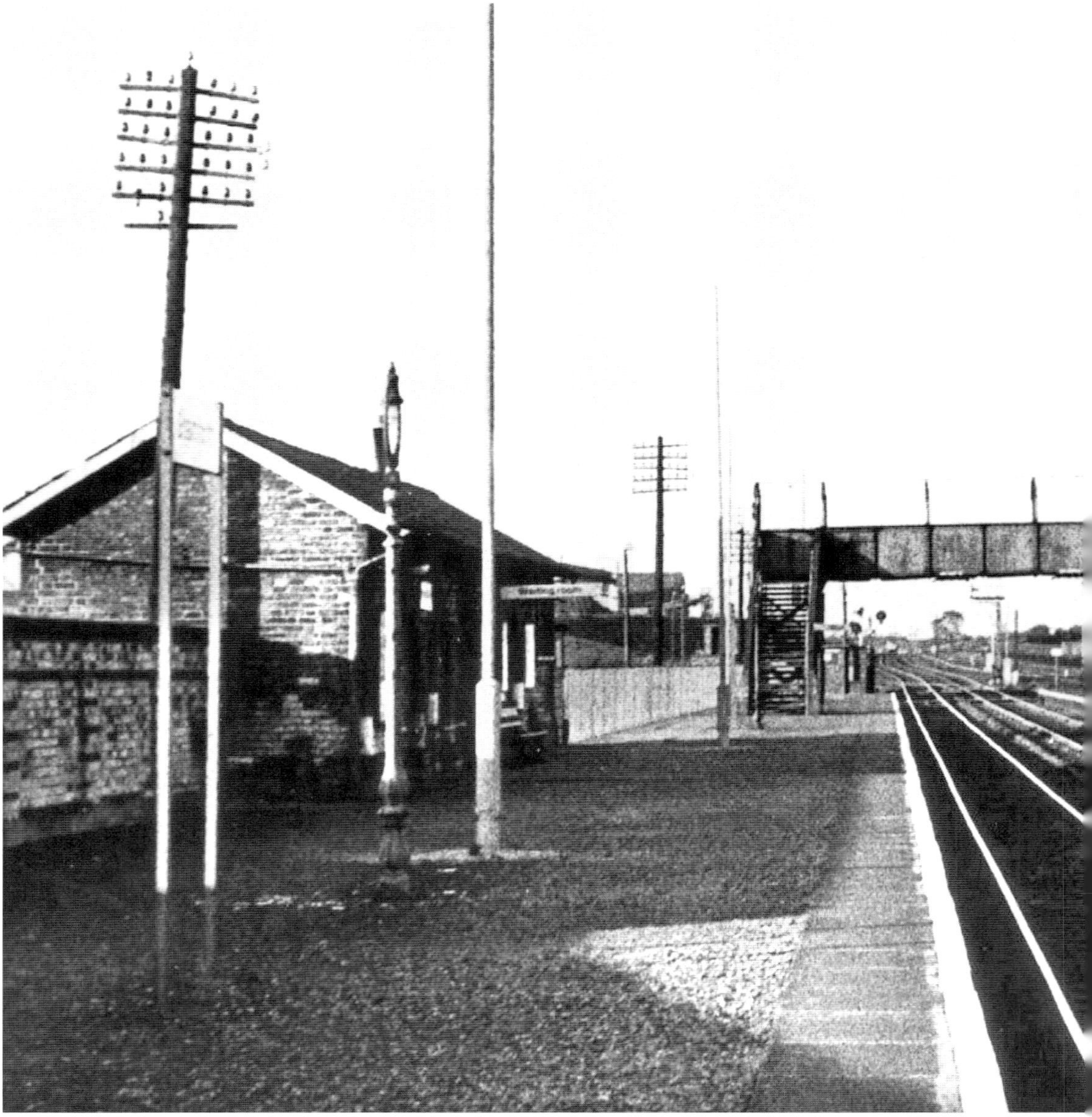

17. This panorama is allowing us to look north on 26th May 1975 and we can find many sidings in the distance. The entrance buildings are on the right. (N.D.Mundy)

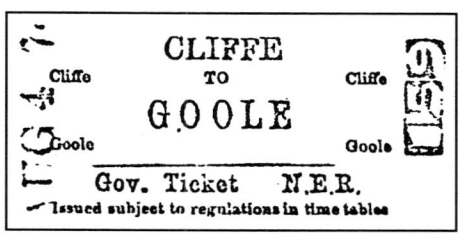

18. Resting on an RCTS Railtour is class D11 4-4-0 no. 62660 *Butler-Henderson*. This was the first of the class to be produced and was completed in 1920. It is on the 'South Yorkshire Rail Tour no.4' on 21st September 1958. (Colour-Rail.com)

19. Between the trains can be seen one of the two platforms, both of which serve the centre two of the four running lines, shown in the foreground. Evident is no. 158787 on 19th October 2007. Also clear is Hatfield Main Colliery, north of the station. The colliery raised its first coal in 1916, when much hand labour was used. In 1967 the Hatfield and Thorne collieries were merged, becoming separate again in February 1978. They were merged again on 1st February 1986. Pit closures took place on 3rd December 1993. A takeover occurred in 2001, but it wound its last coal in 2004. There was, however, a fresh production era in 2007-15. (Colour-Rail.com)

NORTH OF HATFIELD & STAINFORTH

20a. A slipped spoil heap on 13th February 2013 caused closure of all lines until 8th July. The astonishing bending of rails reveals the enormous forces involved. The Aberfan disaster of 1966, in South Wales, was greater, with loss of 124 lives. (Network Rail)

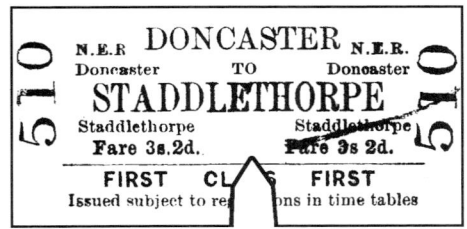

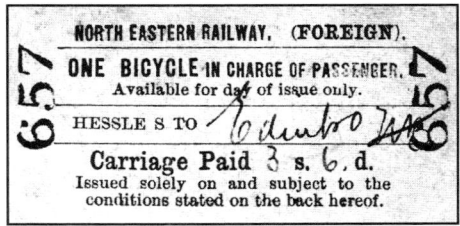

20b. This is the active repair scene on 21st March 2013. The plant visible comprises a Komatsu type PC128 tracked road-rail excavator, a two-seat RTV900, and 11 flat trolleys and trailers. The colliery itself is in the background of this view, also the previous two and the next one. (A.J.Booth)

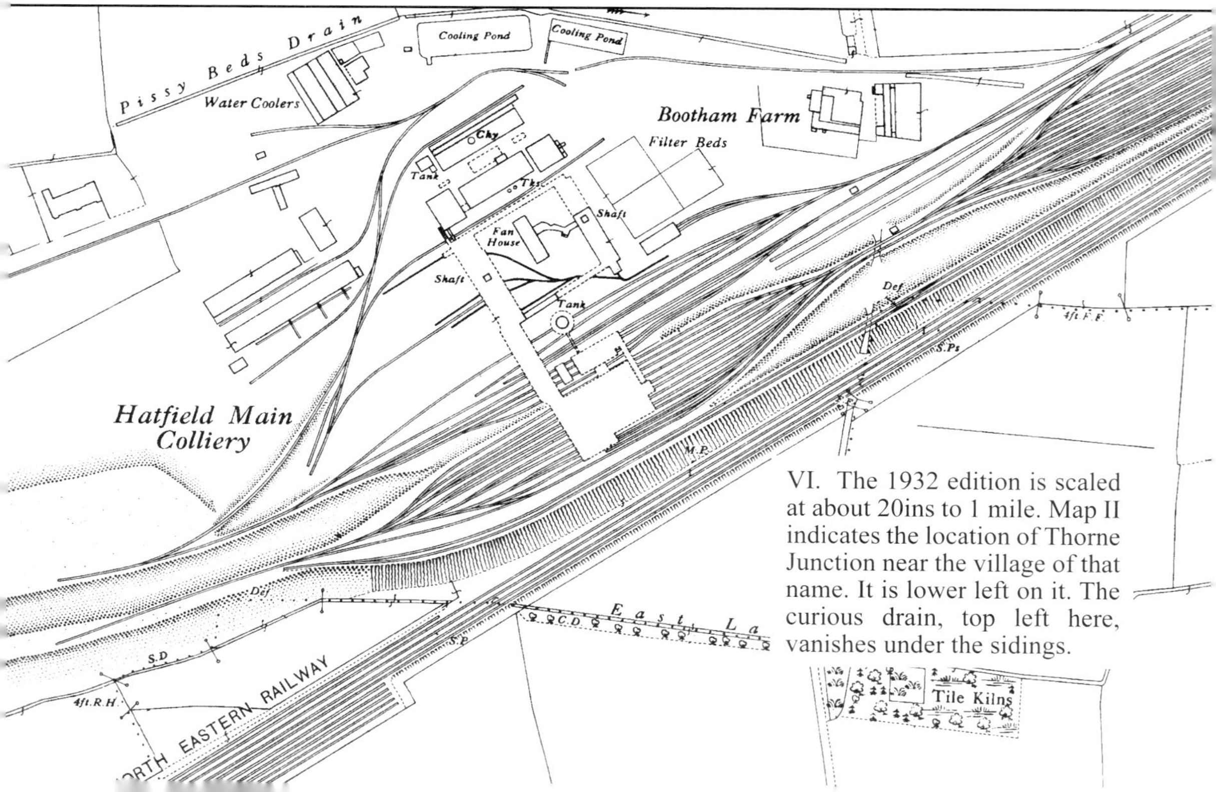

VI. The 1932 edition is scaled at about 20ins to 1 mile. Map II indicates the location of Thorne Junction near the village of that name. It is lower left on it. The curious drain, top left here, vanishes under the sidings.

21. A closer view of the mine has no. 158762 running past, with gold bars on crimson bodies on 12th July 2001. It was the livery of Northern Spirit. The ends were black and yellow. The branding states 'transpenninexpress', with only three 'e's, not four. (Colour-Rail.com)

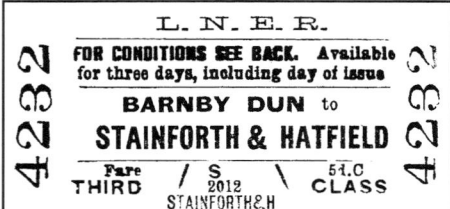

THORNE.
POPULATION, 2,501.
A telegraph station.
HOTEL—White Hart.
MARKET DAY.—Wednesday.
FAIRS.—Monday and Tuesday after June 11 and October 11.
This place contains a population of 2,591 engaged in the rope making, barge building, and carrying trades. The church of St. Nicholas is later English, at which De la Prime, the antiquary, was curate.

Excerpt from *Bradshaw's Descriptive Hand Book*, 1866.

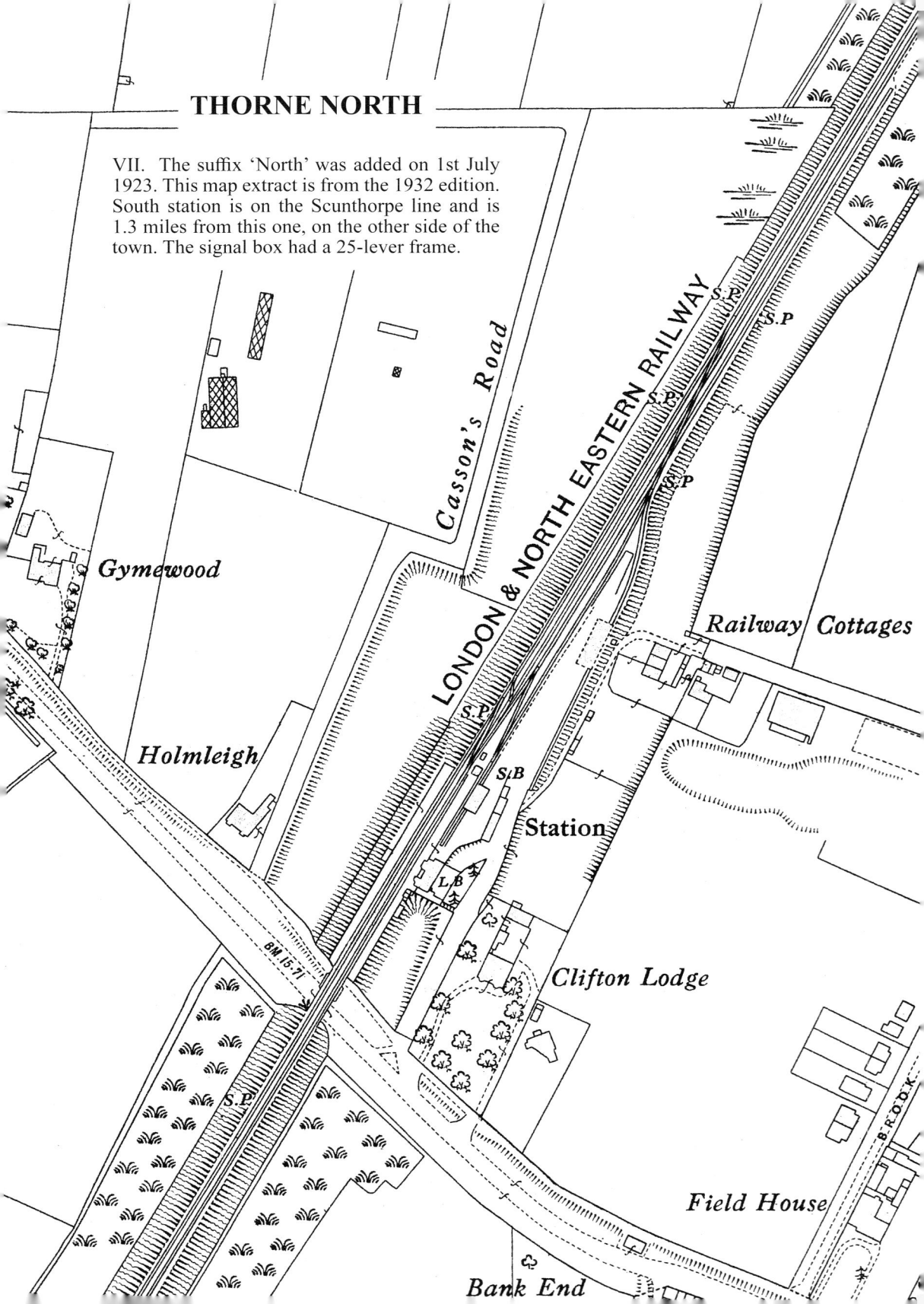

THORNE NORTH

VII. The suffix 'North' was added on 1st July 1923. This map extract is from the 1932 edition. South station is on the Scunthorpe line and is 1.3 miles from this one, on the other side of the town. The signal box had a 25-lever frame.

22. The NER was generous in its provision of footbridges, despite their cost. There were small signal boxes also at Thorne Moor and Thorne Colliery, in the early days. (P.Laming coll.)

23. The staff and some family members pose in a customary manner for postcard producers, in around 1900. The tall pipe is an aid to sewer ventilation. The signal box had 25 levers. (LOSA)

24. The 2.30pm Hull to Doncaster is seen on 1st June 1957. The overgrowth of vegetation since the previous similar view would be partially due to reduced available labour during World War II. No. 61036 *Ralph Assheton* is a class B1 4-6-0 and has just passed the 22-lever signal box. (H.C.Casserley)

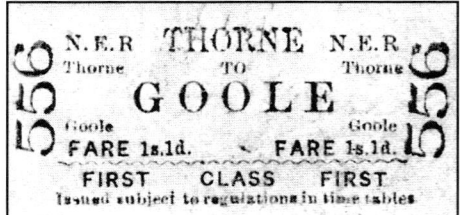

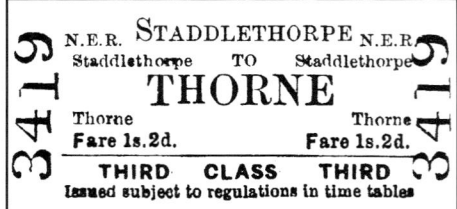

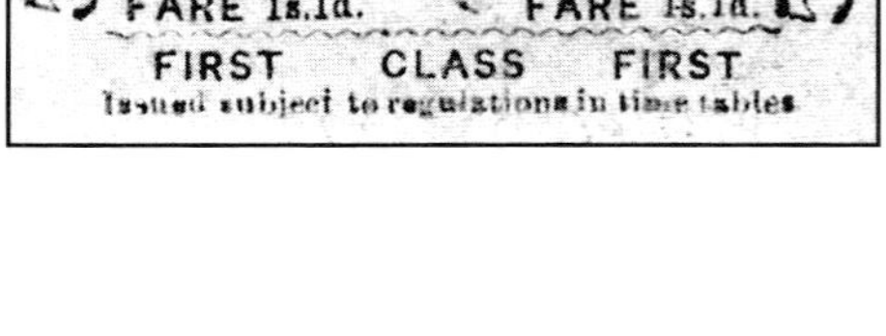

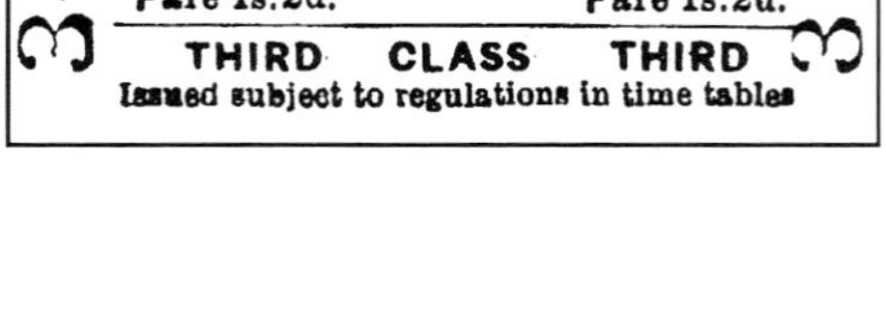

25. We witness a brief flurry of activity at Thorne North – perhaps the busiest moment of the day – on 2nd June 2004, as passengers disembark from the 14.57 Scarborough to Doncaster and the 16.41 Sheffield to Hull. They were formed by units 156479 and 156475 respectively. (P.D.Shannon)

26. No. 142070 is westbound on 10th December 2014 and visibility has improved at last. Even the old lamp has been removed. The goods yard had closed on 5th April 1965; it had a 5-ton crane for years. (A.J.Booth)

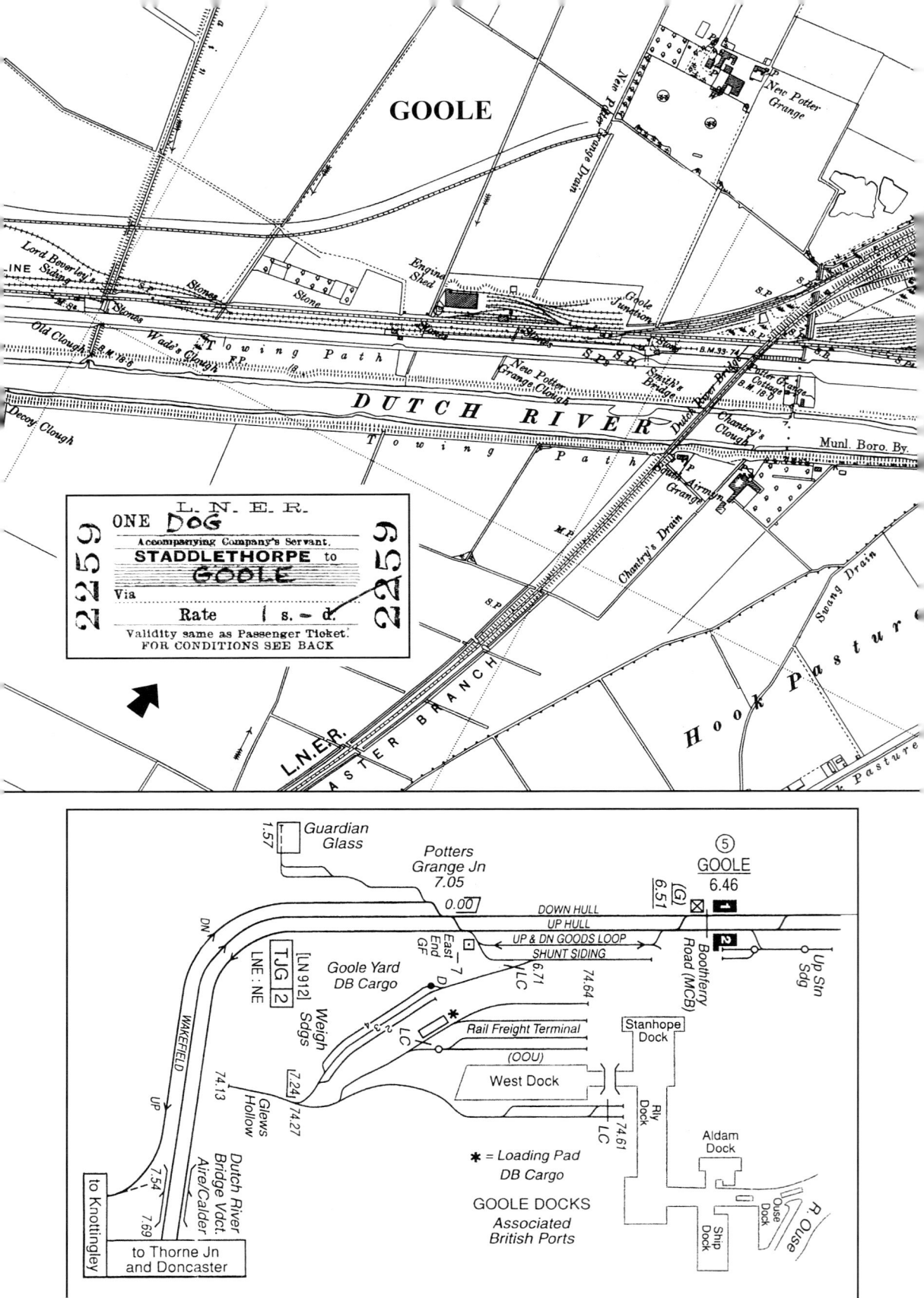

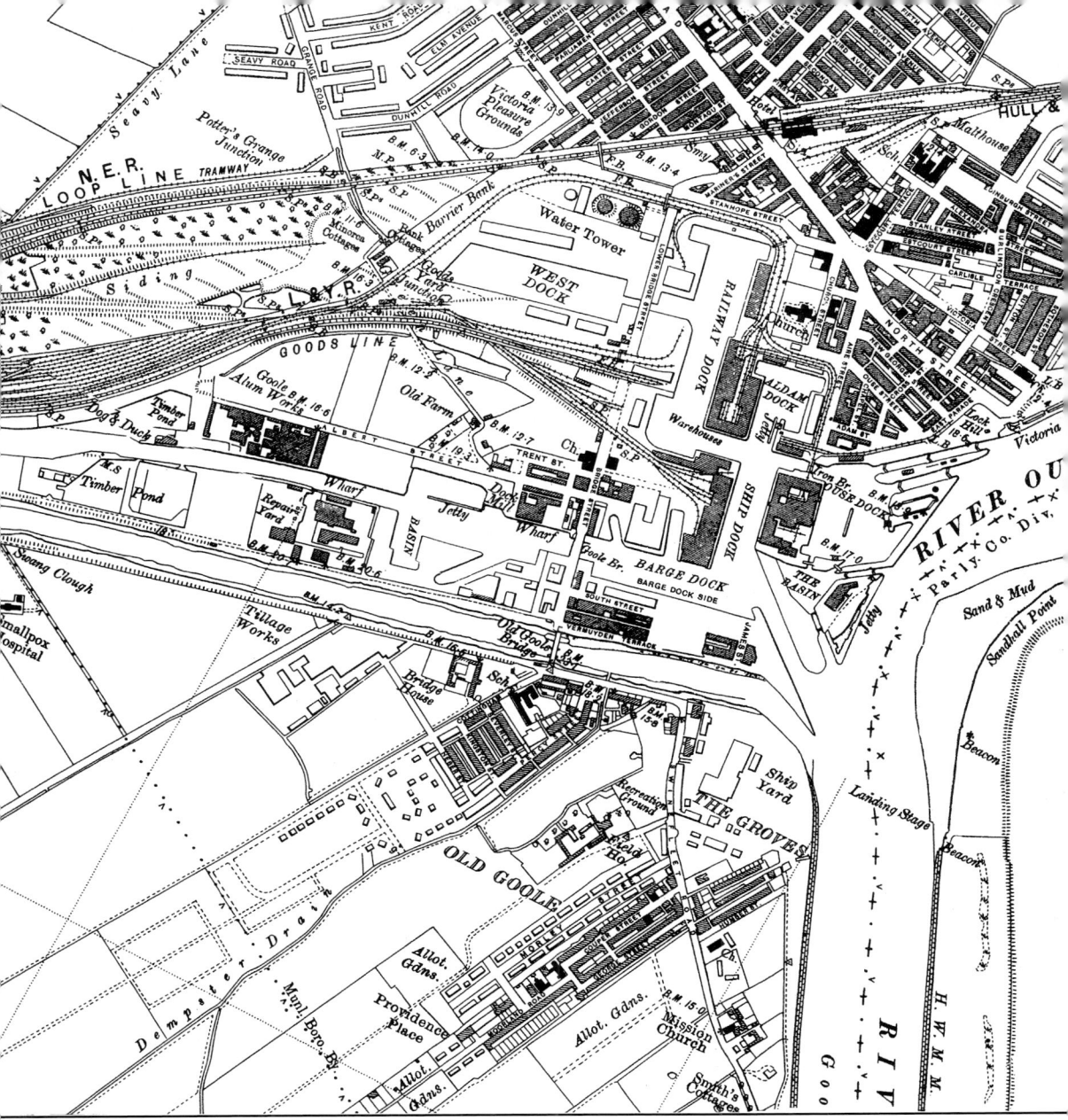

VIII. The 6ins scale map is from 1938 and the TRACKmaps diagram, inset, is dated 2016. We arrive on the line close to it and discover the engine shed, which is above the word 'DUTCH'. This refers to a Dutch canal engineer working here in the 1820s. The line west to the left border goes to Knottingley. This has been used mostly for freight recently. It was also used by Selby trains until 1964. Running beneath it is the canal from Leeds. Two signal boxes are shown left of the page join. Top is Potters Grange Box which opened in 1912 with 25 levers and closed in 1975. Below it is Dutch River box, which had a 55-lever frame when it was closed on 24th February 1974. Goole Goods Junction box opened in 1891 with 40 levers. A new frame came in 1958 with 55 levers. Closure came on 20th June 1989. There was also a small box beyond the lower border in the early days. It was called Marshland. The 2016 diagram, left, has a glassworks top left. This received several loads of sand each week from Middleton Towers, near Kings Lynn.

27. The station is on the right here and top right on the last map. The level crossing is near the hotel on the left. Anglo-American refers to a prominent oil company in the 1900s. (P.Laming coll.)

28. This view is from the level crossing on 22nd April 1959 and features the 7.20am Hull to Doncaster. It is hauled by no. 61250 *A.Harold Bibby*, a class B1 4-6-0. The first was completed by the LNER in 1942. (H.C.Casserley)

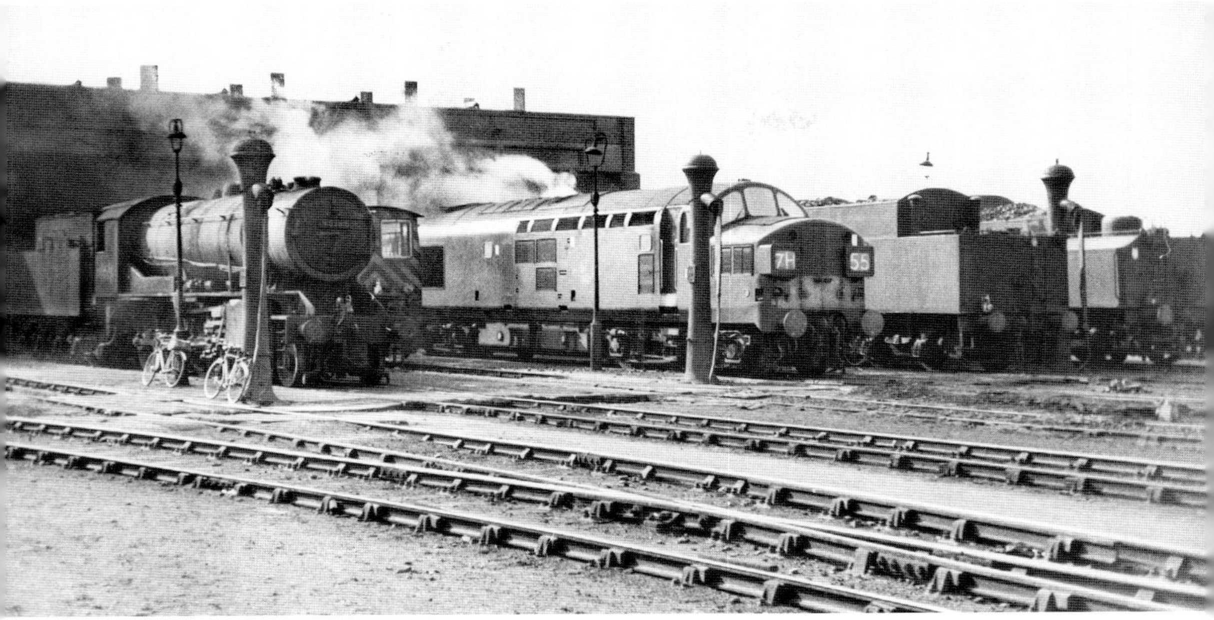

29. The shed here was built by the Lancashire & Yorkshire Railway. This view is from 30th March 1963 and appears to show no. D6733 steaming. Shed codes were 25C from 1948, 53E from 1956 and 50D from 1960. Goole Engine Shed signal box opened on 20th May 1880 with 32 levers. A new frame came in about 1955 with 40 levers. The box closed on 20th May 1980. (T.Heavyside)

30. The coaling tower reveals its lift for loaded coal wagons on the left, in 1968, the year after the shed had closed. Its allocation of locos was 34 in 1950, 27 in 1959 and 13 in 1965. (A.J.Booth)

L&N.E.R. SALTMARSHE L&N.E.R.
Saltmarshe To Saltmarshe
1713 DONCASTER,G.C 1713
Doncaster,G.C Doncaster,G.C.
Via Thorne
Fare 2s.6d Fare 2s.6d
THIRD CLASS THIRD
Issued subject to conditions in current time tables

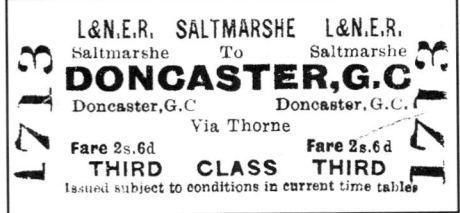

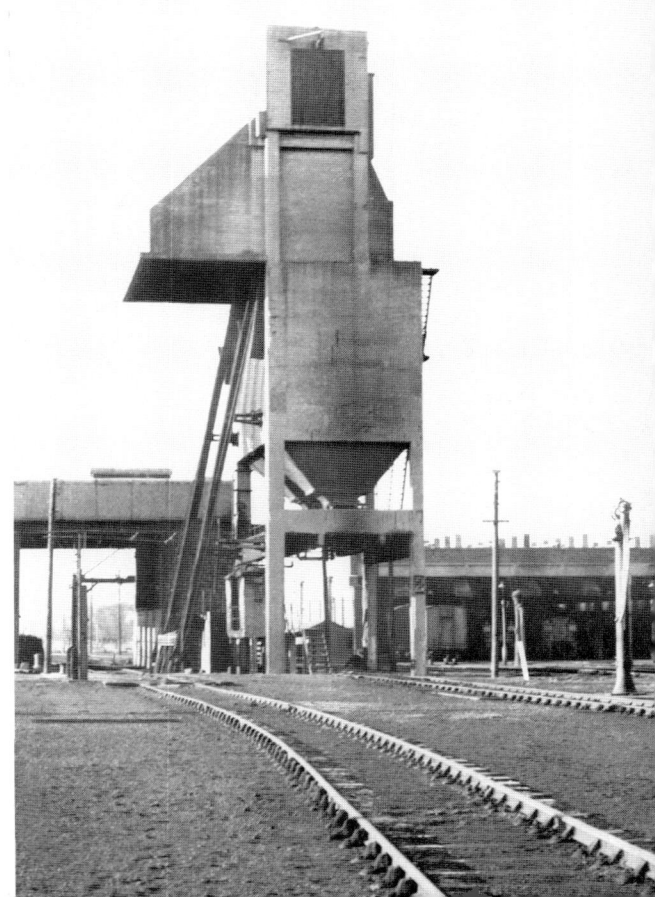

31. No. 55016 *Gordon Highlander* arrives with the 12.05 Kings Cross to Hull on 30th May 1981. The signal box was completed on 31st August 1909, with 51 levers, but the lifting barriers arrived in the 1960s to protect Boothferry Road. A panel is in use now. (T.Heavyside)

32. The prospective passenger's perspective is seen on 23rd November 1987. Goole is famed for being the UK's furthest inland port. For more than 150 years the port was a hub for the export of coal arriving from the Yorkshire coalfields via the canal and railway, until their decline in the 1980s. Engineers developed a system of transporting coal along the canal that was unique to Goole. Compartment boats, nicknamed Tom Puddings (due to their resemblance to a string of black puddings), were linked together in long 'trains' and pulled along the canal by a tug. At the docks, hydraulic compartment boat hoists lifted the Tom Puddings and tipped their contents into the holds of waiting ships. (D.A.Thompson/Middleton Press coll.)

33. The attractively redeveloped station frontage catches the morning sun on 2nd April 2001. By 2020, there was staff present at peak times and a waiting room was then open. Passengers numbered almost 0.3m per annum. (A.C.Hartless)

34. The modern presentation was recorded on 7th May 2010. The L&YR terminated in the dock area from 1st April 1848. The NER's route, which opened on 2nd August 1869, arrived from Thorne at a higher level and bridged over the L&YR. The new station was used by both companies from 1st October 1879. Views of the complex dock area can be found in our *Leeds to Selby and Goole* album. (R.Humm)

EAST OF GOOLE
Goole Bridge

35. DMU no. E56051 passes over the many spans of the swing bridge on 30th May 1981. The signal box upper left opened in 1899 with three levers. It was given 15 in 1911. North Box and South Box had long gone by 1981. Goole also had its own shipbuilding and repair company on the Old Goole side of the Dutch River until the 1980s. (T.Heavyside)

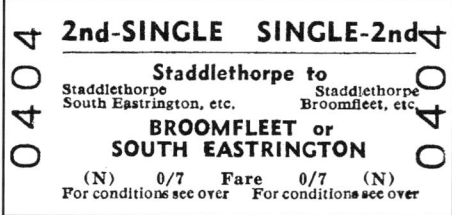

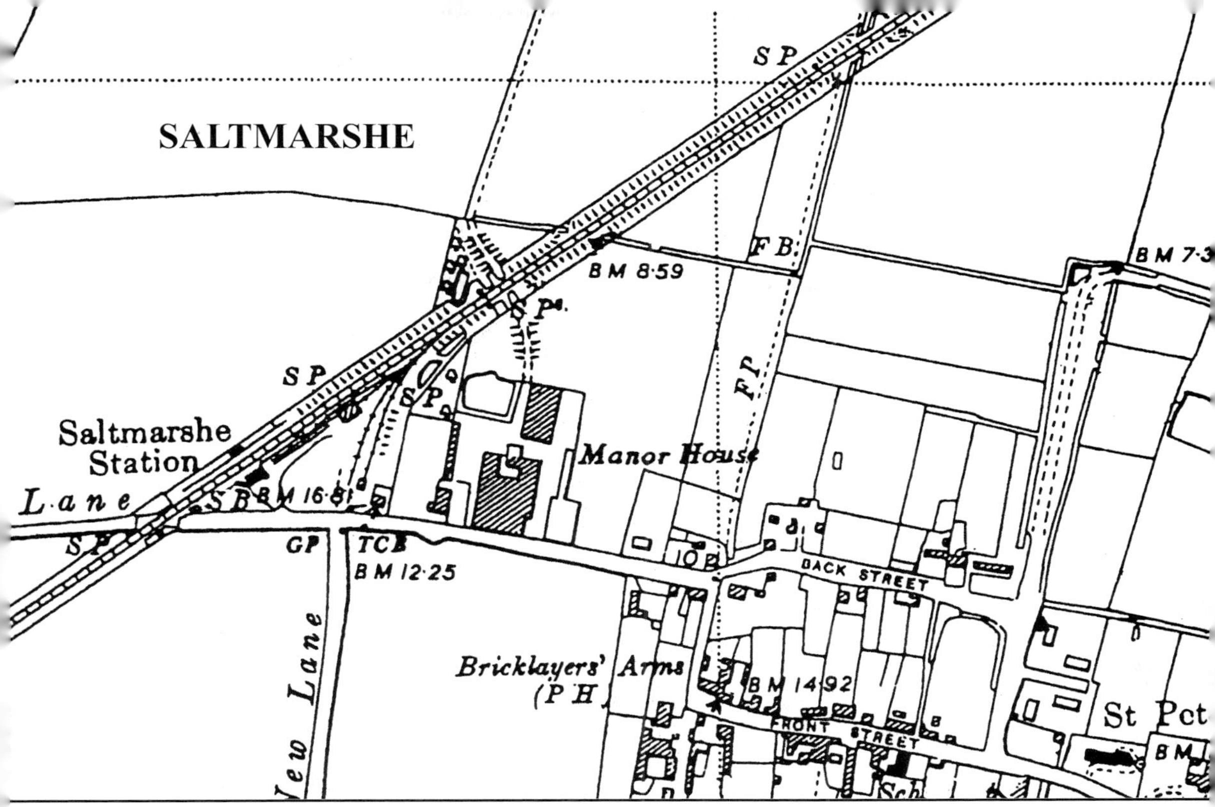

SALTMARSHE

IX. The 1952 edition at 6ins to 1 mile reveals the ground height being 7 to 15ft above sea level. Three sidings are shown in the goods yard, which closed on 4th May 1964. It had a one ton crane in its goods shed.

36. This card was posted in 1905 and reveals staff and families, plus lack of a footbridge. The station opened on 2nd August 1869 and is still in use. (P.Laming coll.)

37. This signal box opened in 1905 with 29 levers. The frame was shortened by 1972 to 20 levers. Running by on 23rd March 1957 is class B1 4-6-0 no. 61289, with the 10.20am Kings Cross to Hull. (R.Humm coll.)

38. A close-up of the box on 9th February 1973 reveals evidence of the new colour light signalling system. The sign above the coal store confirms that there was still no footbridge. An oil lamp is still in use on the left. The box was closed on 26th November 2018. (R.Humm coll.)

39. A view from 18th September 1980 reveals the unusual angled corner of the signal box. This was to enable the signalman to see if any traffic was approaching, as the road was at an angle. (D.A.Thompson/Middleton Press coll.)

WEST OF GILBERDYKE

40. In the distance is the straight line running direct towards Selby since 1840. Reference to map I can help. Running on the curve, on 30th May 1981, is no. 55013 *The Black Watch* with the 08.05 from Kings Cross to Hull, last stop Goole. (T.Heavyside)

41. No. 31411 in 'white stripe' livery passes Gilberdyke Junction with the 09.41 Manchester Victoria to Hull train on 25th July 1984. A number of Class 31/4s were outshopped from Finsbury Park with a white stripe in the late 1970s - a rare deviation from the strict BR corporate image of the time. (P.D.Shannon)

42. DBS no. 66156 runs past on 11th June 2018. It is in EWS livery and is working the 10.27 Milford West Sidings to Hull, with biomass stock. The box was built in 1903 as West Box, with a 55-lever frame. It closed on 26th November 2018. (R.J.Stewart-Smith)

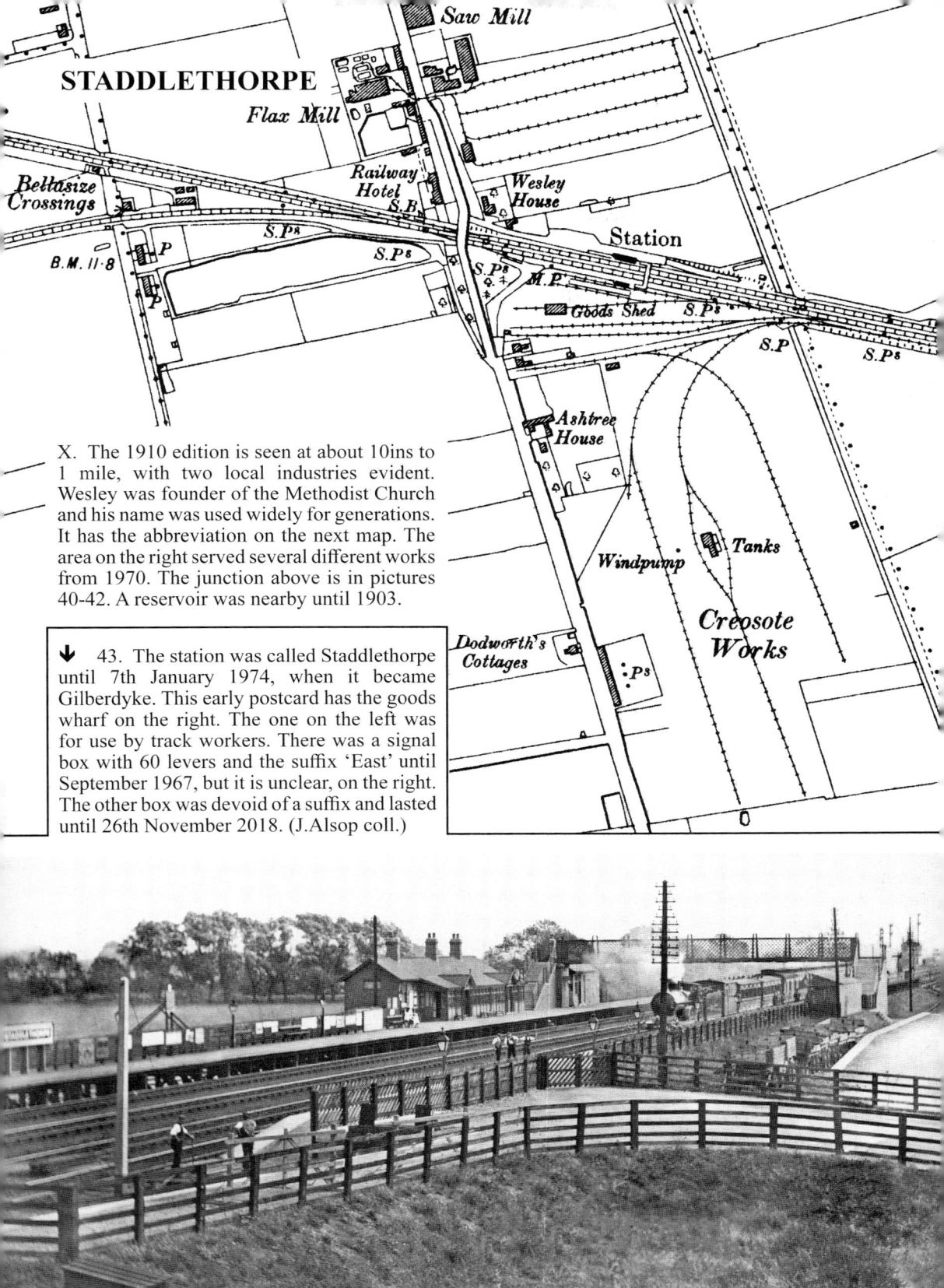

X. The 1910 edition is seen at about 10ins to 1 mile, with two local industries evident. Wesley was founder of the Methodist Church and his name was used widely for generations. It has the abbreviation on the next map. The area on the right served several different works from 1970. The junction above is in pictures 40-42. A reservoir was nearby until 1903.

↓ 43. The station was called Staddlethorpe until 7th January 1974, when it became Gilberdyke. This early postcard has the goods wharf on the right. The one on the left was for use by track workers. There was a signal box with 60 levers and the suffix 'East' until September 1967, but it is unclear, on the right. The other box was devoid of a suffix and lasted until 26th November 2018. (J.Alsop coll.)

GILBERDYKE

44. No. 31445 passes Gilberdyke at speed with the 11.05 from Hull to Lancaster on 25th July 1984, while a Class 114 unit - cars E54015 and E53001 - pauses for custom with the 10.56 stopper from Hull to Sheffield. The four tracks between Gilberdyke and Broomfleet were reduced to two in 1987 and the platforms were rebuilt. (P.D.Shannon)

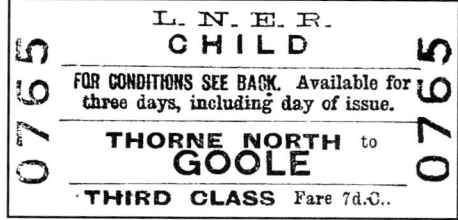

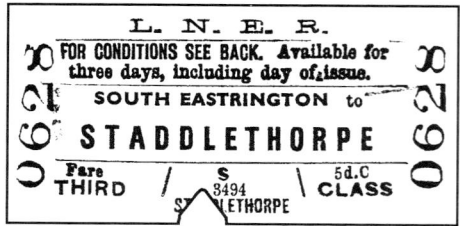

45. There are traces of the goods yard, which was closed on 3rd May 1965. It had three sidings and a 5-ton crane. It is April 2001 and no. 66150 is signalled for the Goole line as it passes with the 14.36 Hull Docks – Doncaster. Broad Lane bridge provides the vantage point. The track at the right was by now a tamper siding. (A.C.Hartless)

46. Class 185 no. 185137 departs on 11th June 2018. The platform ramps have been replaced by fences. The 10.40 from Hull Paragon to Manchester Piccadilly was run by TransPennine Express. (R.J.Stewart-Smith)

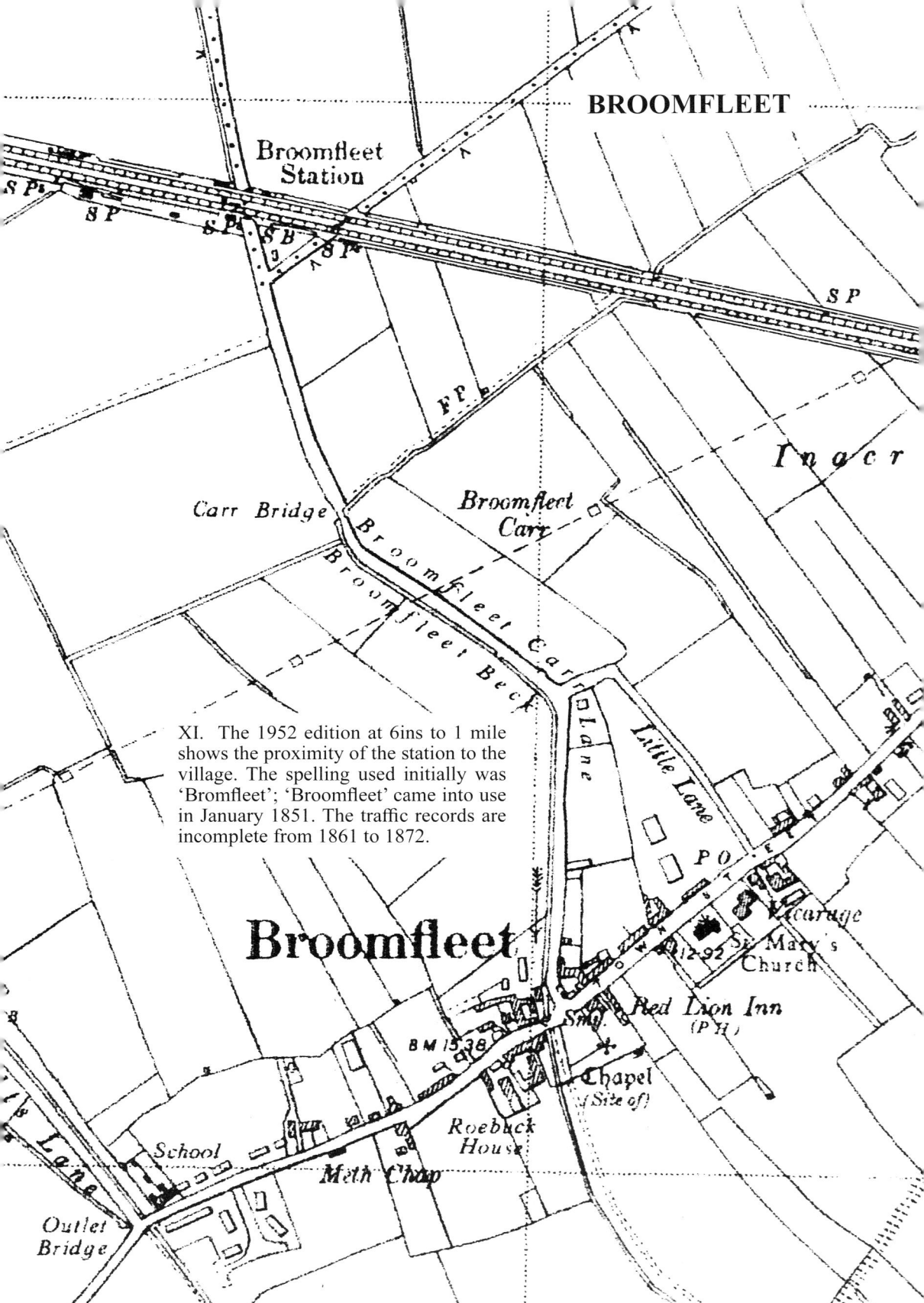

XI. The 1952 edition at 6ins to 1 mile shows the proximity of the station to the village. The spelling used initially was 'Bromfleet'; 'Broomfleet' came into use in January 1851. The traffic records are incomplete from 1861 to 1872.

47. Until October 1907, the service was erratic, often just Tuesdays, which was market day locally. This view east is from about 1939. The 1904 signal box had 60 levers. It was reduced to a gate box when the line was resignalled in November 2018. Further east there was Cave Crossing Box until that date. The loco is a class B16/1 4-6-0. (Stations UK)

48. It is 12th April 1962 when the first batches of DMUs were adorned with decor widely termed 'Cats Whiskers'. A much older treat is to see a glass mantle still surrounding an oil lamp wick. The signal box was opened in 1904. (R.Humm coll.)

49. The station was situated ½ mile from a brick works and over a mile from the Humber. The DMU seen on 8th July 1967 now has the universal yellow ends. The goods yard closed on 4th May 1964. (R.Humm coll.)

50. Entering the four-track section at Broomfleet on 25th July 1984 is no. 40056 with the 15.54 Speedlink train from Hull to Aberdeen Craiginches. This train called en route at York Dringhouses, Tyne Yard, Millerhill and Dundee. (P.D.Shannon)

51. It is 2nd April 2001 and a pair of single cars in Regional Railways livery, nos 153352 and 153331, run past with the 09.40 Sheffield to Hull. The station stands in lonely farmland ½ mile from its village. There were four tracks here when traffic was busier; the lightweight platforms were constructed on the formation of the two outer lines. The waiting shelters mark the alignment of the original platforms. The emergency crossover was subsequently removed. In 2014-18 the annual passengers numbered circa 1350. Staffing ceased in 1976. (A.C.Hartless)

CRABLEY CREEK

52. There was a station here from 1844 to 1861, by which time the number of agricultural labourers was diminishing in favour of mechanisation. A class 185 passes over the public footpath on 6th May 2017. This led to the Humber shore. The 1891 signal box had 45 levers from 1904 to about 1956, when there were only 12. Closure came on 26th November 2018, for signalling only. There was a legal requirement in the deed for control of road traffic over the crossing. In 2020 a lady was often in charge; she had to keep her eyes on a screen with a map of the line, showing how far away the approaching trains were from Crabley Creek. (J.Whitehouse)

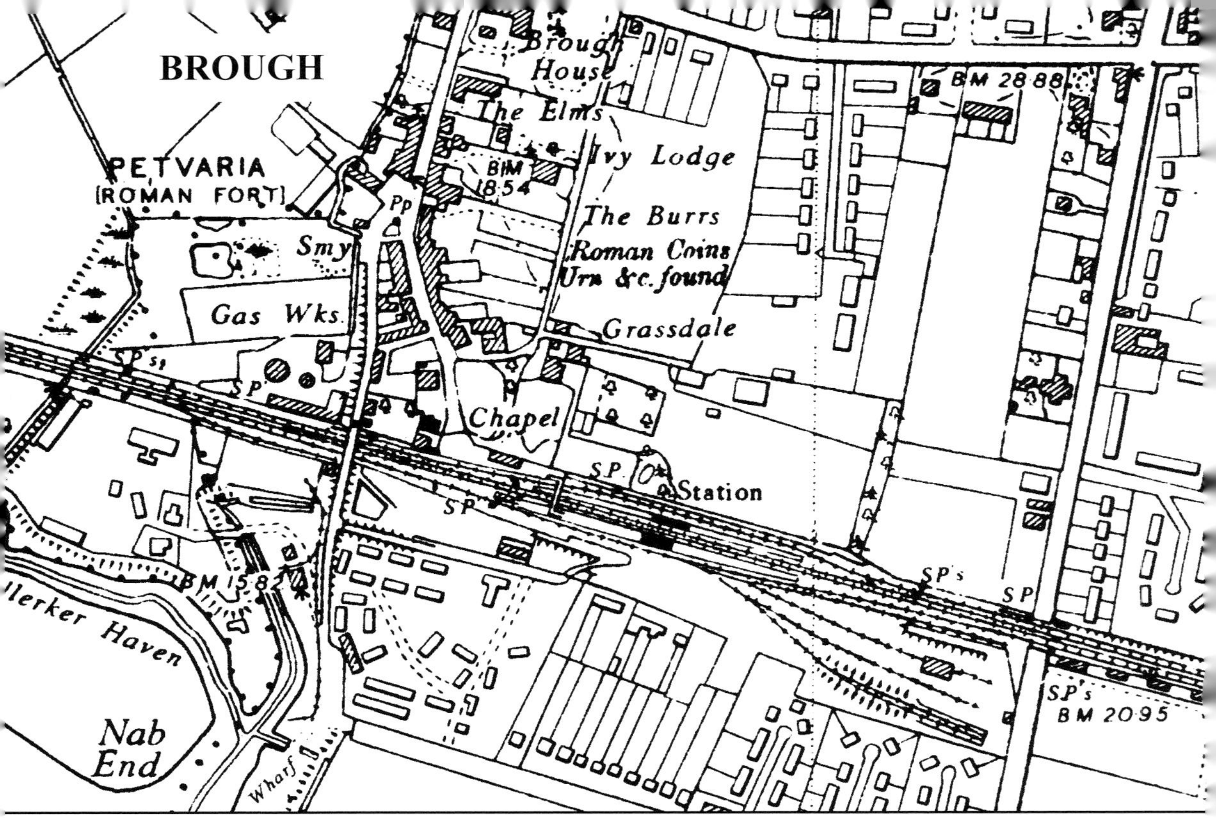

XII. The 1952 edition at 6 ins to 1 mile shows access to the Humber, if you can cope with the mud to reach the wharf. Coal for the gas works would have probably arrived by barge. It opened in 1871 and closed in 1948. Annual coal tons used rose from 607 in 1900 to 2400 in the final year.

53. This view east has the station adorned about 50 years after it opened. The goods shed is still on the north side and the creeper-covered sign on the left states just GENTLE. The cattle wagon has a lime washed base, for hygiene reasons. (J.Alsop coll.)

54. This card was printed in 1895 and shows an increase of creepers and details of the ornamental chimney pots. Even the gutters were obstructed. The station was just east of the London to York Roman Road, Ermine Street; see map II. There is a memorial on the waterfront to three ferry boats that crossed the Humber in the Bronze Age. These boats were recently unearthed. (J.Alsop coll.)

55. The coming of quadruple track in 1904 meant that a new station had to be created east of the original one. We are on one of the two island platforms, soon after their completion. (P.Laming coll.)

56. There was a travelling post office on the route leaving Hull at 8.40pm and running to Leeds, from 1903 until 1917, when it became just a mail train. This was the only location on our route where a mail bag was collected at speed. A pick-up arm was east of the station. There were sorting offices on the train in the early years. (J.Alsop coll.)

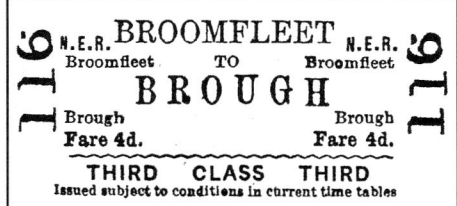

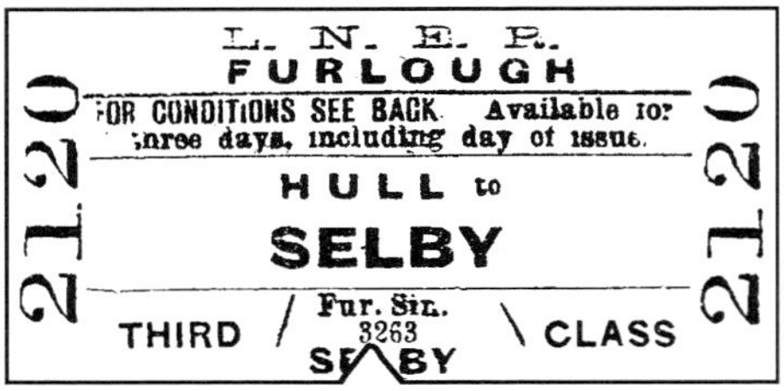

Brough Aircraft Factory

The Blackburn Aeroplane and Motor Company, incorporated in 1914, established a new factory here in 1916. The works was rapidly producing seaplanes for the allied forces during World War I, and the Humber River would prove to be a convenient test facility.

During the mid-war years, Brough concentrated on the continued production of torpedo bombers, seaplanes and patrol aircraft, creating many designs for consideration and use by the Fleet Air Arm. The two-seater Bluebird was made in this period. The Reserve Flying Training School was built in 1937. The control rooms were above the second floor. An engine builder arrived in 1934.

With the outbreak of World War II, Brough intensified its production of the Botha light bomber/trainer and, latterly, the Fairey Barracuda naval torpedo bomber. Between 1949 and 1957 the runway and airfield Perimeter Road became a motor race track.

The main users subsequently are: Blackburn Aircraft Ltd (1958), Hawker Siddeley Aviation (1963), British Aerospace (1977) and BAE Systems (1999). Much extra passenger traffic was generated over the years, particularly for Forces Furlough tickets.

It is claimed that Brough is Britain's oldest remaining aircraft factory.

57. West Box and the long footbridge are seen on 18th May 1964 as the 2.46pm Hull to Sheffield Midland leaves. There had once been a private siding nearby, serving a timber yard. The box had 20 levers when opened in 1874. The man, top left, is changing the oil lamp on the signal. (R.Humm coll.)

58. A train from Hull arrives on 26th July 1980, as many enjoy the extended shelters. On the right is the goods shed and deserted yard, which had closed on 5th November 1970. The class 37 has end doors. (T.Heavyside)

59. We have three photos from 11th March 1982 in our survey. The retired goods offices are present in this unusual starting point for us. The awning was of value when loading goods into road vehicles in bad weather. (D.A.Thompson/Middleton Press coll.)

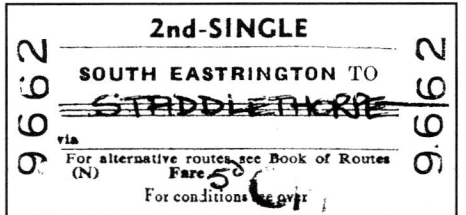 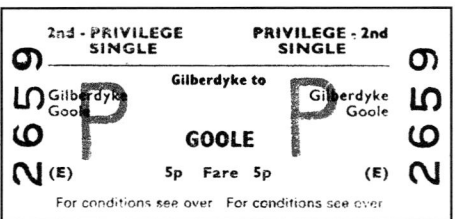

60. This path gave access to the station from the road, near the right border of the map. The booking hall was in the original building, shown below the 'ap' of 'chapel'.
(D.A.Thompson/Middleton Press coll.)

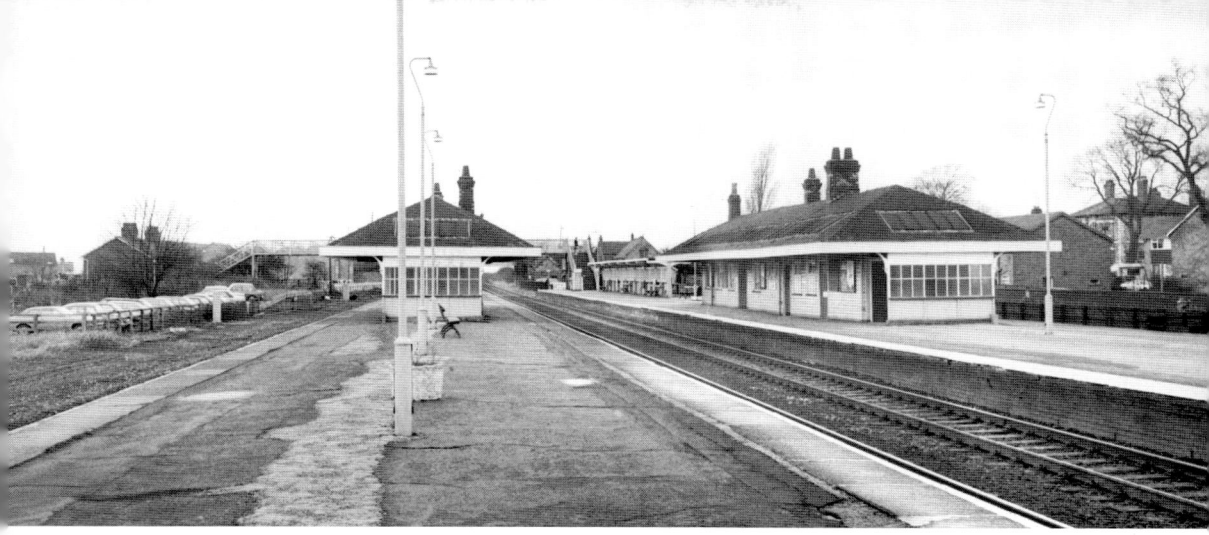

61. Some dwellings of Grassdale are on the right, while the site of the goods yard is on the left. It had the benefit of a crane with 3-ton capacity. To the left of the photo was Brough Aerodrome. It did not have any rail access but was served for years by the Brough Workman's Trains, two daily in each direction. (D.A.Thompson/Middleton Press coll.)

1142 2nd- SPECIAL CHEAP SINGLE SPECIAL CHEAP SINGLE -2nd 1142

Eastrington to

Eastrington Howden | Eastrington Howden

HOWDEN

(N) For conditions see over | (N) For conditions see over

L.N.E.R. SPECIAL SINGLE TICKET.

Not Transferable. This ticket is issued subject to the General Notices, Regulations & Conditions in the Coy's current time tables. Available on day of issue only

STADDLETHORPE to

NORTHHOWDEN

Fare 6d.

THIRD S.S.T NoHowden CLASS

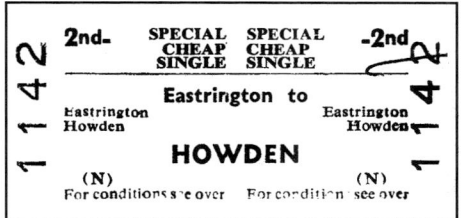

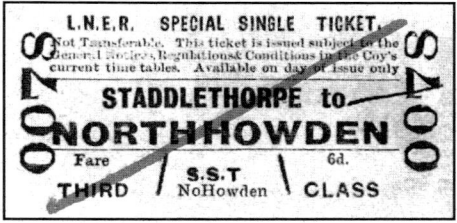

62. Cravens Class 105 cars E54431 and E51288 pass Brough East signal box while working the 14.43 from Hull to Doncaster on 25th July 1984. The box with its 52-lever frame opened in 1904 and closed on 26th November 2018, along with most other boxes on the line. (P.D.Shannon)

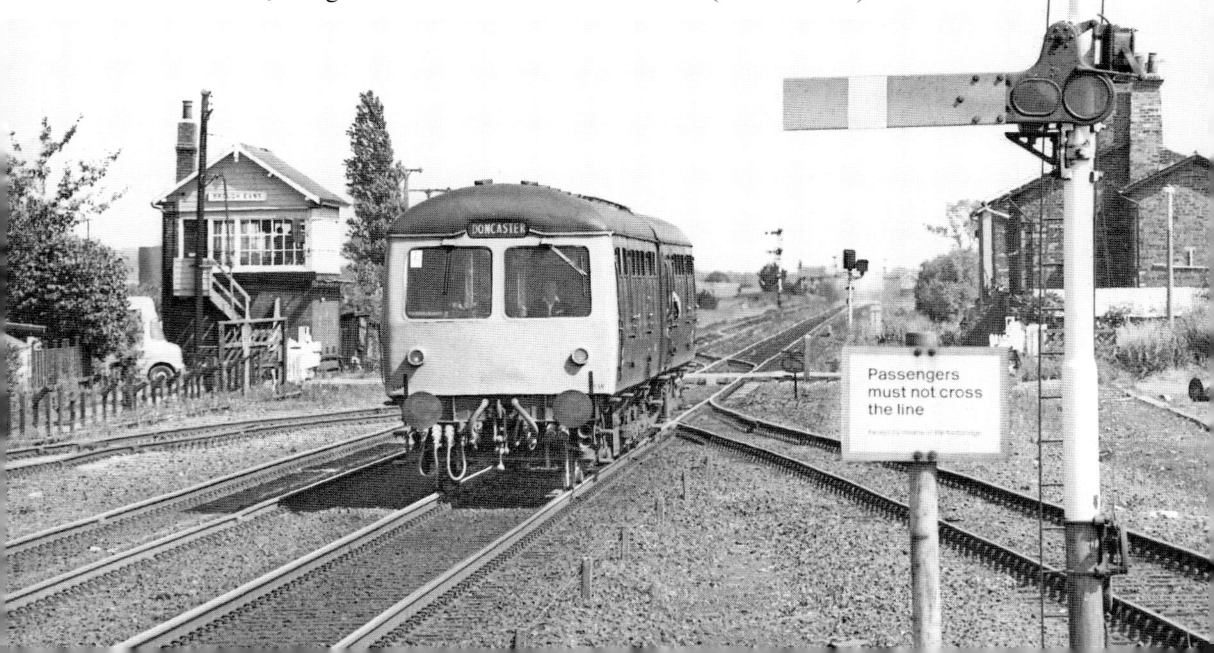

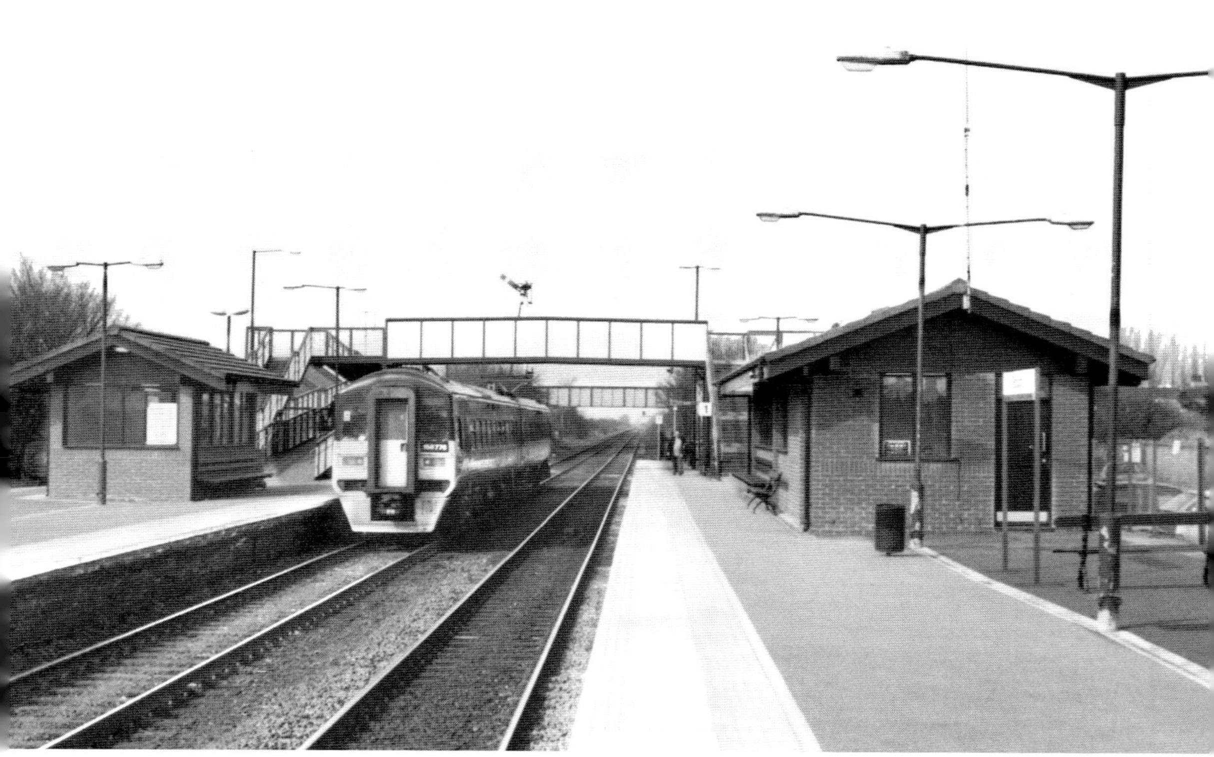

63. It is 2nd April 2001 and no. 158776 departs with the 09.49 Scarborough–Manchester Airport. We see the footbridge which has both steps and ramps in the modern manner. (A.C.Hartless)

64. The first ever TransPennine Express to call here was running from Manchester Piccadilly to Hull on 18th July 2013. Passenger numbers here were over 0.46m by 2018, annually. (J.Whitehouse)

2nd - SINGLE SINGLE - 2nd
0072 0072
Hessle to
Hessle Melton Halt
Hessle Melton Halt
MELTON HALT
(N) 1/0 Fare 1/0 (N)
For conditions see over For conditions see over

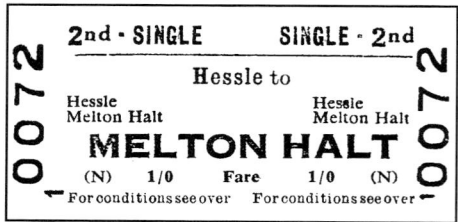

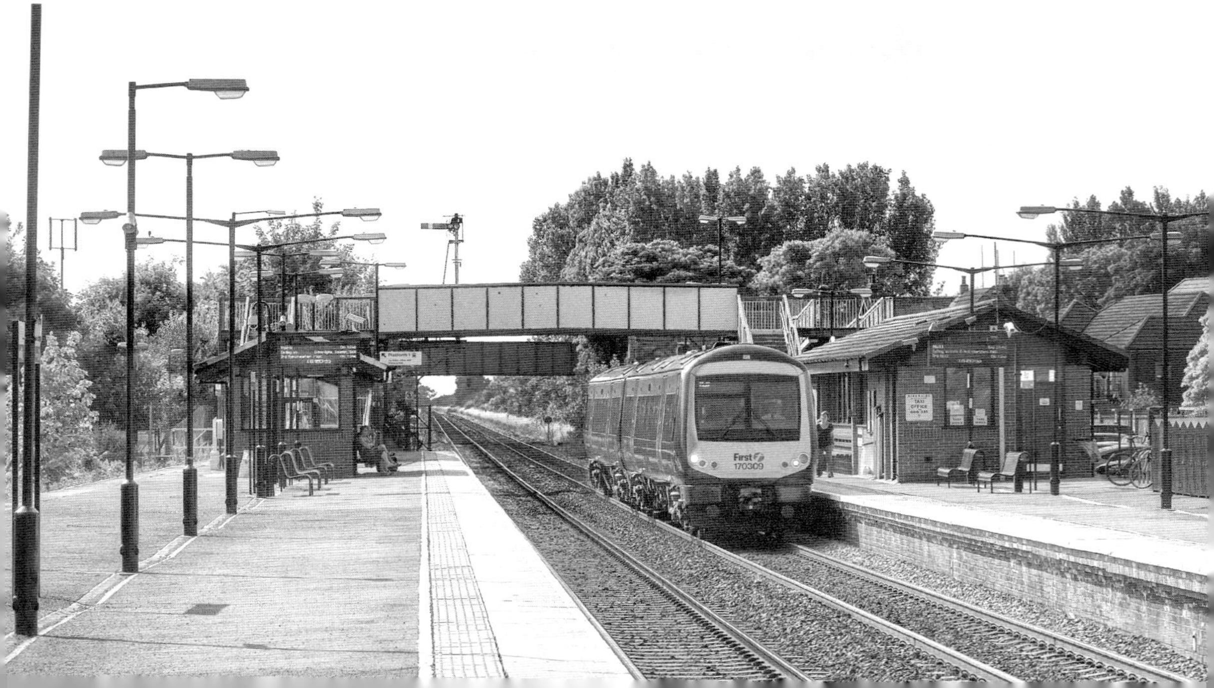

MELTON HALT

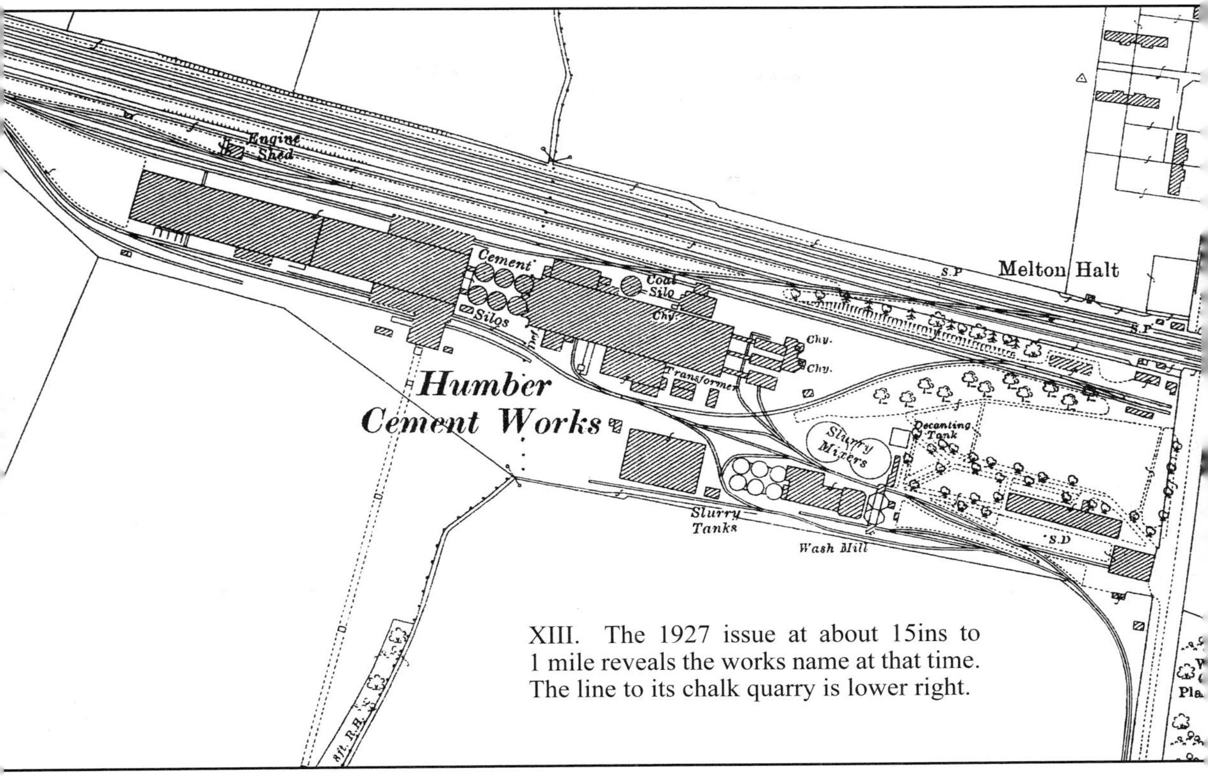

XIII. The 1927 issue at about 15ins to 1 mile reveals the works name at that time. The line to its chalk quarry is lower right.

65. It is 17th June 1960, with class D49/2 no. 62763 *The Fitzwilliam* on the 5.53pm Hull to Doncaster. On this occasion it was only a short train, being usually 8-9 coaches. Melton Halt opened in 1920 and was used to serve the staff at Capper Pass Cement and Smelting Works, which was adjacent. It does not appear in public timetables and was only served by a few local trains. After closure of the works, the halt closed on 8th July 1989. (P.Harrod)

66. No. 142089 is passing the one remaining platform on 6th May 2017. The small gate was for railway staff only. At the time of construction the line through Melton Crossing Halt had four tracks. When the eastbound slow line was lifted in the 1970s, a short wooden platform was provided alongside the former fast line on the east side of the level crossing. The 1904 box had 34 levers and lasted until 26th November 2018. (J.Whitehouse)

67. When seen on 18th February 1984, the site was operated by Blue Circle Industries. The neat single-road locomotive shed was of red brick construction, with a corrugated iron roof and a roller-shutter door. On this date it housed Ruston & Hornsby no. 513139 of 1967. (A.J.Booth)

WEST OF FERRIBY

68. John Fowler Ltd of Leeds built this little 0-4-0 diesel mechanical shunter, fitted with a front-jackshaft drive, to their works no. 22060 of 1937. It is seen on 16th May 1979 at the works of Capper, Pass & Son Ltd of Ferriby. This was a smelting and refining company specialising in non-ferrous refining, particularly tin. Originally established in Bristol, the firm relocated to Ferriby in the 1930s. At its peak the plant produced 10% of the world's output, but the works closed in 1991. (A.J.Booth)

69. Class B1 4-6-0 no. 61075 is with the 3.40pm London fish train from Hull on 15th July 1960. The booked time of departure varied. It ran non-stop to Peterborough, where, on this day, examination took place and some vans were taken off. The booked time for the journey was 5h 8min. It often ran 30 minutes early, as soon as the fish vans were loaded. (P.Harrod)

FERRIBY

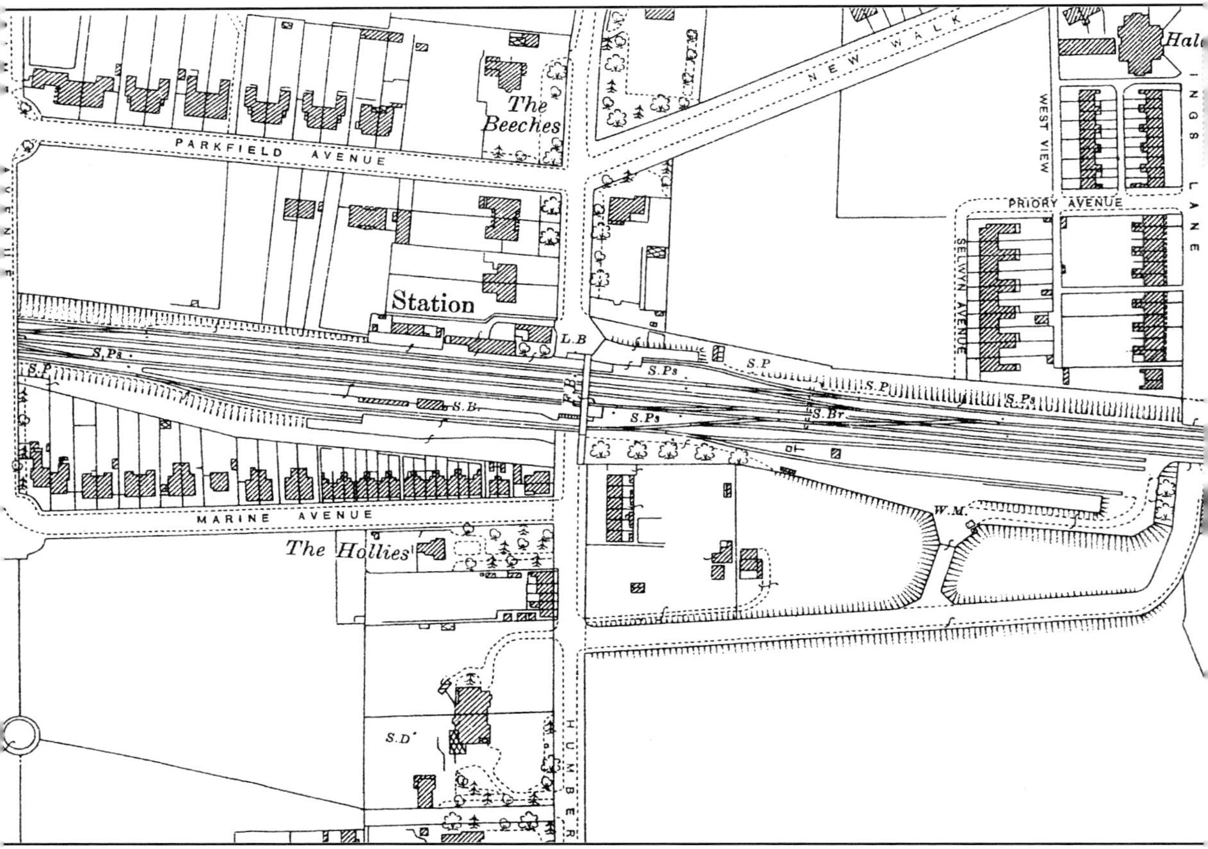

XIV. The 1927 survey is at 20ins to 1 mile and features the extensive goods facilities, which were in use until 3rd May 1965. There was no crane, but a signal box is shown. It had 70 levers and was worked until 26th July 1980.

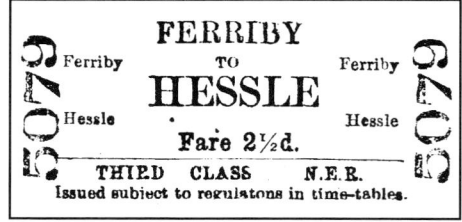

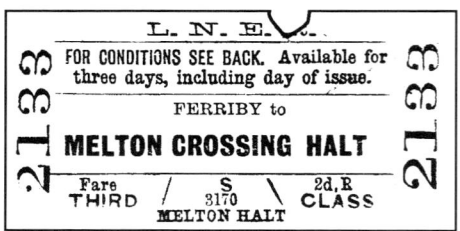

70. The locality was known as North Ferriby, but the station never was. The population in 1901 was just 167; in 2001 it had risen to 3819. The two main buildings appear in the next view. The wooden building was in use by a supplier of kitchen fittings in 1999. (J.Alsop coll.)

71. The track on the right had been retained to serve the cement works. It also saved making a new platform. Westbound on 3rd August 2005 is no. 66952 working for Freightliner. The station was unstaffed by that time, but had around 40,000 passengers annually. (A.J.Booth)

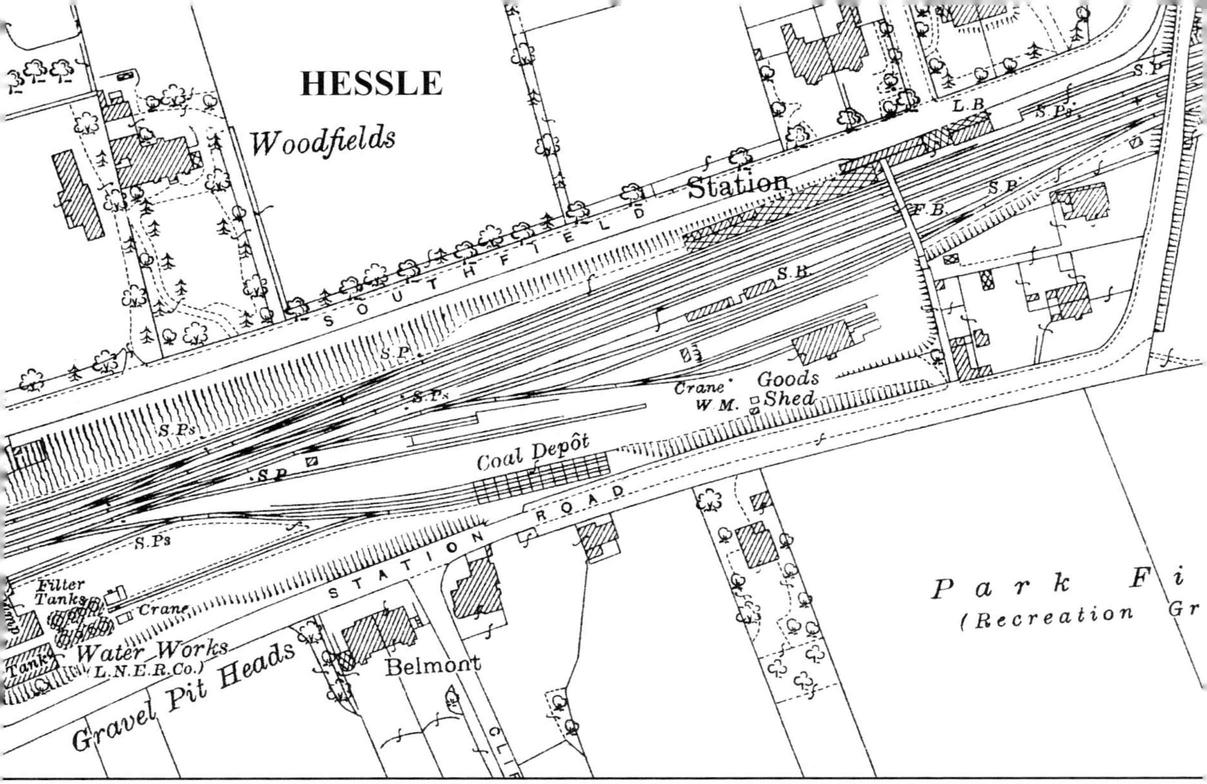

XV. The 1927 map shows Station Road to be remote from the entrance buildings, a rare mistake. Lower left is the LNER's water supply.

72. This is a rare pre-1904 view of just two tracks. The 1901 census recorded 3754 living here. The hoop on the left is at the foot of a sack truck, for parcel and case traffic. The new station was built west of this one. (J.Alsop coll.)

73. A panorama from the new footbridge records the new platform, on the left, and a fresh approach to the goods yard. All goods trains were loose coupled in those early years. (J.Alsop coll.)

74. This image shows the other line to give access to the goods yard. It also contains two of the water filter tanks and a set of catch points. (Stations UK)

75. The date is 18th May 1964 and we are looking towards Hull, with two road bridges beyond the footbridge. The goods yard had a 5-ton crane and closed on 4th December 1967. There were three private sidings listed in 1938. The 80-lever signal box was in use until 22nd October 1972. There was a smaller box at Hessle Haven and another for Hessle Quarry sidings. (R.Humm coll.)

76. It is 30th March 2015 and Northern's Pacer unit no. 142023 arrives with the 13.52 Doncaster–Hull. The Humber Bridge, ½ mile to the west, overlooks the scene. It opened on 24th June 1981; the nearby station details are in our *Branch Lines North of Grimsby* album. Notice how much this platform had been widened during the track reduction. Passengers numbered over 40,000 per annum at that time and have exceeded 50,000 since. (A.C.Hartless)

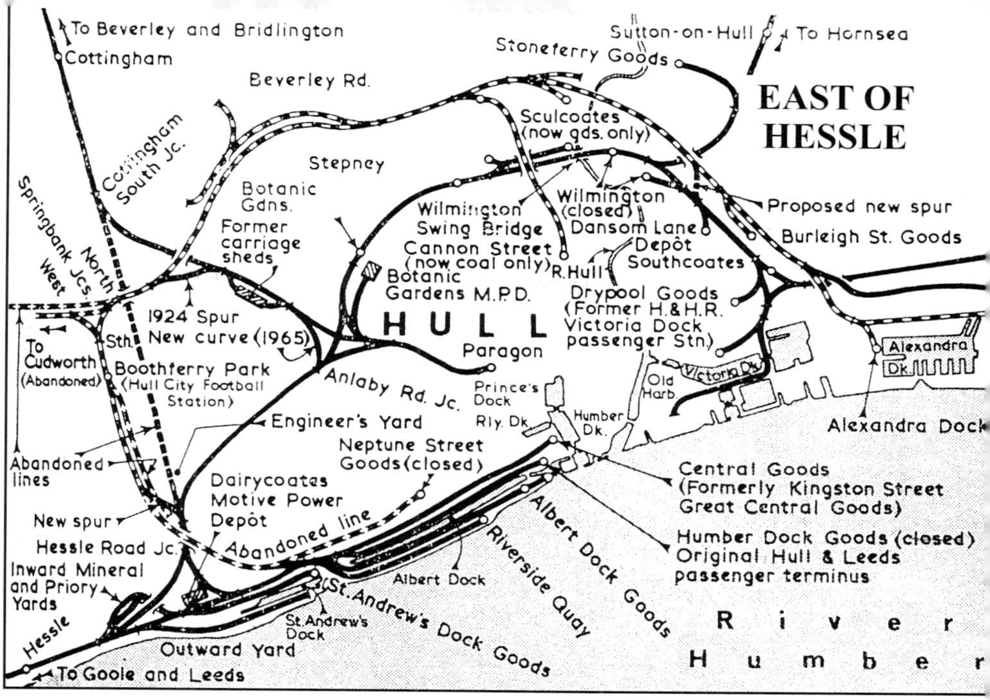

XVIa. The dockland in 1923 is shown, together with earlier railway companies. Paragon station is below **HULL** in this 1967 diagram. (*The Railway Magazine*)

↓ XVIb. Hessle Hump Marshalling Yard opened on 9th December 1936 in the form seen. It was limited to 3mph and the 4-8-0T humping engine could propel up to 47 wagons to the top of its 1 in 18 slope. (*The Railway Magazine*)

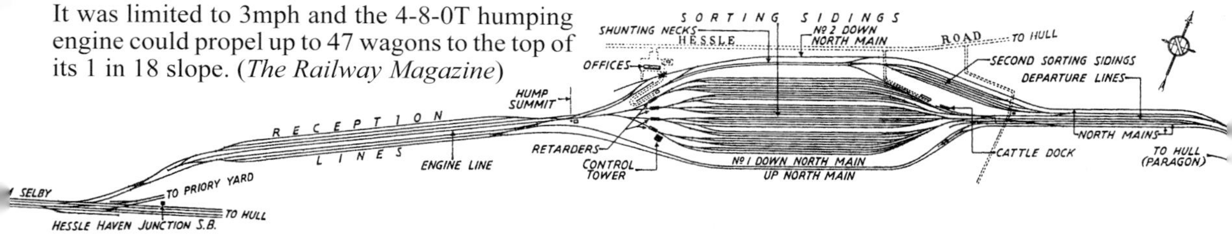

77. 0-8-0 class Q6 no. 2218 nears Hessle in 1933. The siding on the right was coming in from the shipyard on the West Bank of Hessle Creek. This yard, owned by Livingstone & Cooper, closed in 1922, but the siding was in theory still served by a D class goods in 1933. The site was totally cleared by 1938. (T.Routhwaite/P.Harrod coll.)

HESSLE EAST JUNCTION

78. The signal box had 60 levers and lasted until 11th July 1965. On 18th February 1961, WD no. 90099 gains the main line at Hessle Junction from the Outward Yard, with what appears to be a coal train. This is odd, as coal was normally brought into Hull from collieries in West Yorkshire. It may have been for local sidings and stations, which were served by westbound trains. Since the closure of the full Hull and Barnsley line in April 1959, coal trains from West Yorkshire used the Leeds to Hull line. On the right is the siding serving the North Eastern Gas Board Hessle Gas Works. This continued in use for a few more years. (P.Harrod)

79. Class D49/1 no. 62722 *Huntingdonshire* is at Hessle Haven with the 5.53pm train to Doncaster on 19th August 1959. This was non-stop to Goole; over 23 miles to be covered in 30 minutes. Quite hard going for a 4-4-0 which had spent the winter in store at Springhead shed. The passenger loco shed in Hull, Botanic Gardens, had closed to steam in June 1959. The eight D49s had been transferred to Dairycoates. (P.Harrod)

WEST OF HULL
St. Andrews Dock

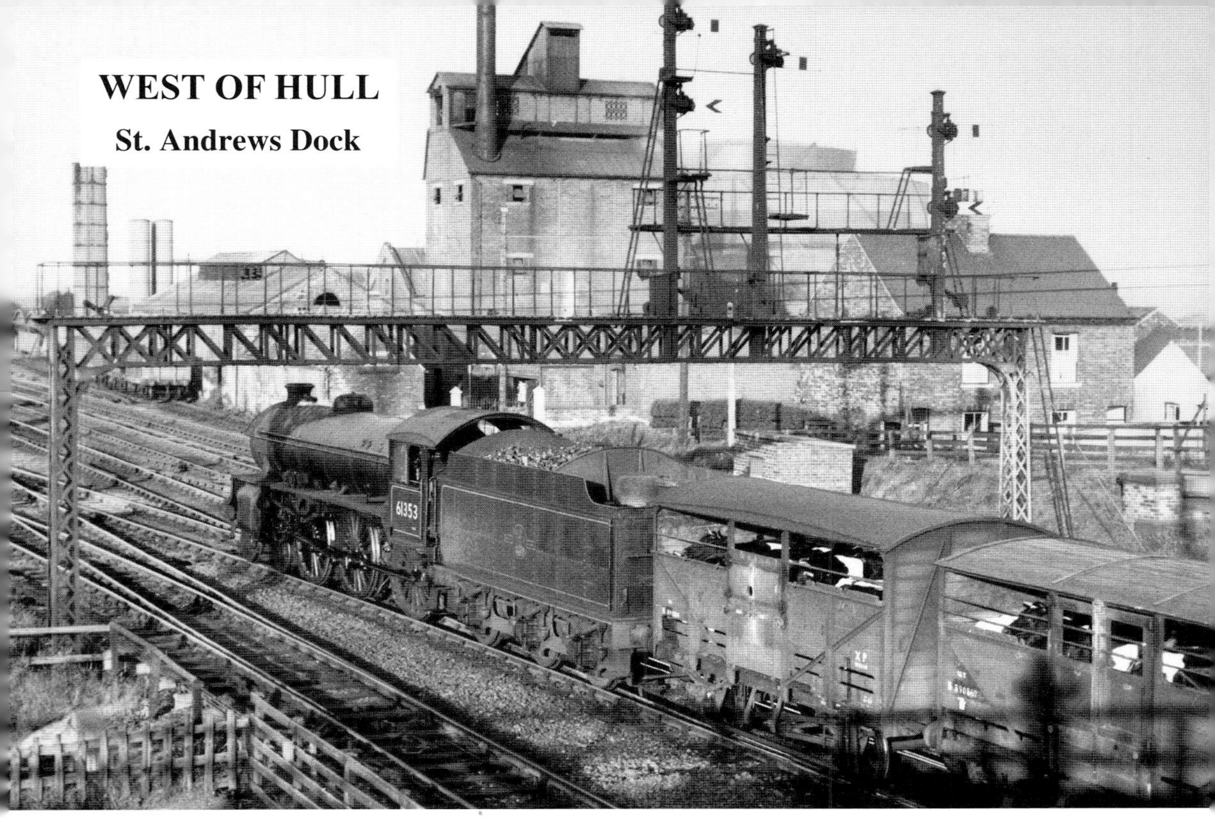

80. Class B1 no. 61353 heads into Inward Yard with a cattle train on 22nd May 1959. Hessle Gas Works siding is on the right. Gas was made from 1860 to 1964. 1460 tons of coal was used in 1900, increasing to around 7900 per annum in the 1950s. The white patches belong to the animals and the gaps in boards were to aid clearance of their droppings. (P.Harrod)

81. The dock is shown near the join in the next map. Its shunter in 1958 was class J77 0-6-0T no. 68414. It carries the shed code 51D, which refers to Middlesbrough. Its duty no. is 22. The shed closed in 1958. (Transport Treasury)

Riverside Quay

82. This was opened in 1908 by the NER to enable passengers to transfer to boats to the continent. Trains could run directly from the west or from Hull Paragon station. As many as 20 trains per week used the station, which was in use until 1938. Destroyed by bombing in WWII, it was reopened in 1946 using Mulberry Harbour sections. By 1953, it was no longer an embarkation site, but the sidings were used to serve cranes loading, mainly. This is shown on the right of the right-hand page of the next map. (J.Alsop coll.)

83. Consent was given for a quay of up to 5580ft in length, that could dredge to a depth of 16ft below the low water level of ordinary spring tides. The quay was designed as a deep water one for foodstuffs and other goods requiring rapid handling. It avoided delays in entering locks, or having to wait for a low tide to turn. (R.Humm coll.)

84. By 1953, Riverside Quay and its box were out of use. Even the signal arms had been removed. A visitor waves a cloth as he poses for a photograph. The clock tower was dignified, as ever. It was of value to ferry operators and other mariners. (P.Harrod)

Hessle Road

85. This road is across the left page of the next map, which was printed over 50 years before this photo was taken in December 1965. Thus the tracks do not relate to it in detail. The DMU has run across the right page from Paragon station and is probably bound for Selby, across the left one. The road had earlier been a turnpike and became the A63 in 1919. Its level crossing was replaced by a flyover in 1962. The line coming in from the left is the old Hull and Barnsley railway line, which, before the rebuilding of the site, crossed the other lines by a bridge. The line coming in from the centre was the Cottingham cut-off line, enabling both goods and passenger trains to access the lines from Hull to York and Bridlington, avoiding reversing at Paragon Station. This line was closed and subsequently replaced by a very short spur at Anlaby Road. (Colour-Rail.com)

XVII. This 1928 edition at about 4ins to 1 mile reveals how much railway progress had been made in about 70 years. Details are included in many of the captions. An exception is the Hull Springhead Engine Shed (top left), which is due in our *Barnsley to Hull* album. It closed in 1958. St. Andrews Dock is on the left of the right page and was created on land reclaimed from the Humber in 1883. It was expanded in 1890. Hull had steadily grown west as seen, and continued to do so later. A church was opened in 1902 and a cinema arrived in 1912, but closed in 1959. This is when Hull had one of the biggest fishing industries in the UK. It soon suffered a rapid decline, plus a great loss of life at sea. Hull once despatched more than 24 trainloads of fish a day to all parts of Britain. By 1977, it was receiving 1000 tons of fish a week by train from the West Country for conversion into fish meal. The fish were carried in block trains of 24-ton stone hopper wagons. The transit time was about 48 hours. A further decline was due to other east coast ports to the south making provision for the expanding container traffic. The docks are worthy of close study here and on the next map. Their siding mileage had grown to 163 by 1930.

KINGSTON UPON HULL

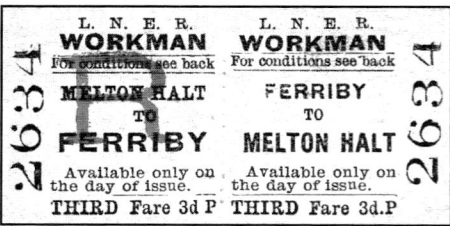

For further views
of this area see
*Hull to Hornsea &
Withernsea.*

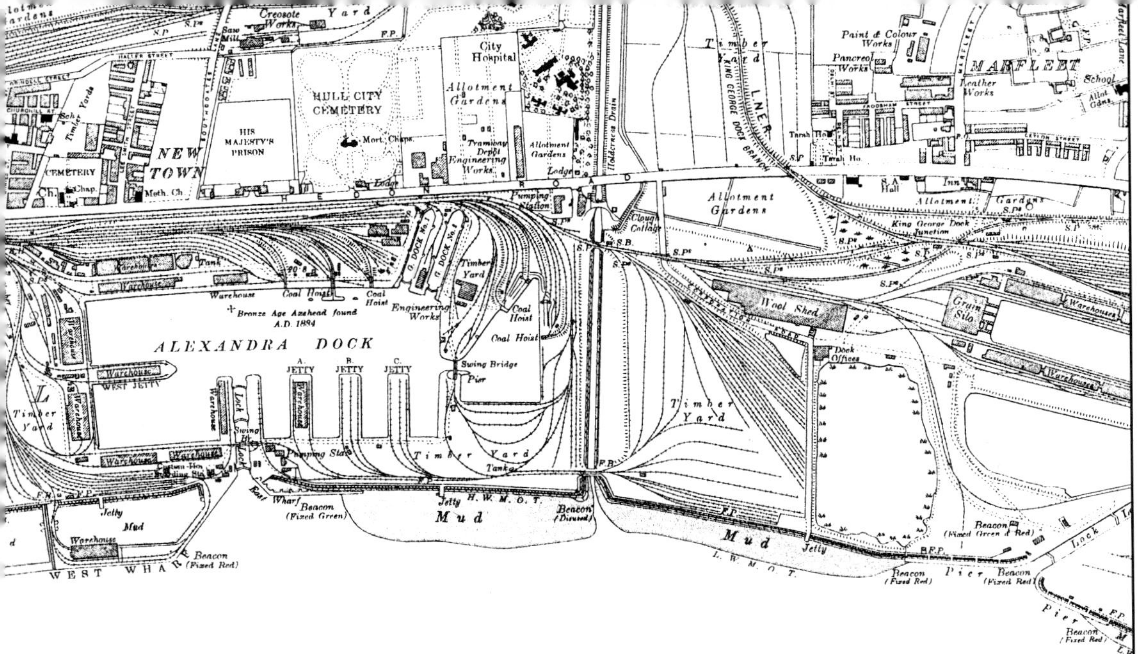

XVIII. These two maps continue from the previous pair and are intended to emphasise the extent of railway development in Hull by 1911. They continued further east. Victoria Pier can be found on the left, near the mouth of the River Hull. The big goods shed is lower left. In March 1967 it was announced that all the level crossings would be abolished within 18 months. Too many cars were being used. Six crossings were removed and one was delayed. Two domestic coal concentration depots were created in 1968-69, eliminating 10. Signal boxes hereon in their final form were: Hessle Road - 83 levers to 1961 (panel from 2008); Anlaby Road - 23 to 1964; West Parade - 120 to 1980; Park Street - 32 to 1939 and Hull Paragon - 143 to 1939. The signalling here was electrified in 1936-39.

86. Victoria Pier received passenger trains from 1st June 1853 until 1st June 1864; see left of the view. It was busy with ferries across the Humber, until the bridge opened. (R.Humm coll.)

Hull Dairycoates Engine Shed

87. The first shed was begun in about 1863 and the site was later to have one of the biggest NER sheds. It was named after an early local farm. In 1950, the shed code was 53A and it housed 145 locos. By 1959, the figure was down to 54. (Colour-Rail.com)

88. When the shed was expanded, it was fitted with six internal turntables of the type seen here. This and the previous picture were taken on 24th July 1960. By then the code was 50B and the allocation was 35. (Colour-Rail.com)

89. Diesel nos D9548 and D9552 were recorded on 12th August 1968. By 1965, there were 24 ex-WD 2-8-0s in residence. Shed closure came in 1970. A tall coaling plant had arrived in 1916. The third shed was called Botanic Gardens and is above the 'H' of HULL on the diagram near picture 77. The latter closed in 1959 to steam engines, but continued as a shed until January 1987 when it became just a refuelling point. (A.J.Booth)

Anlaby Road Crossing

90. This main road traverses the right page of map XVII, after picture 85, and here we witness the enormous gate length needed to protect the highway. The tram tracks were fitted with trap points on their approach to the railway, but the camera is between them. (P.Laming coll.)

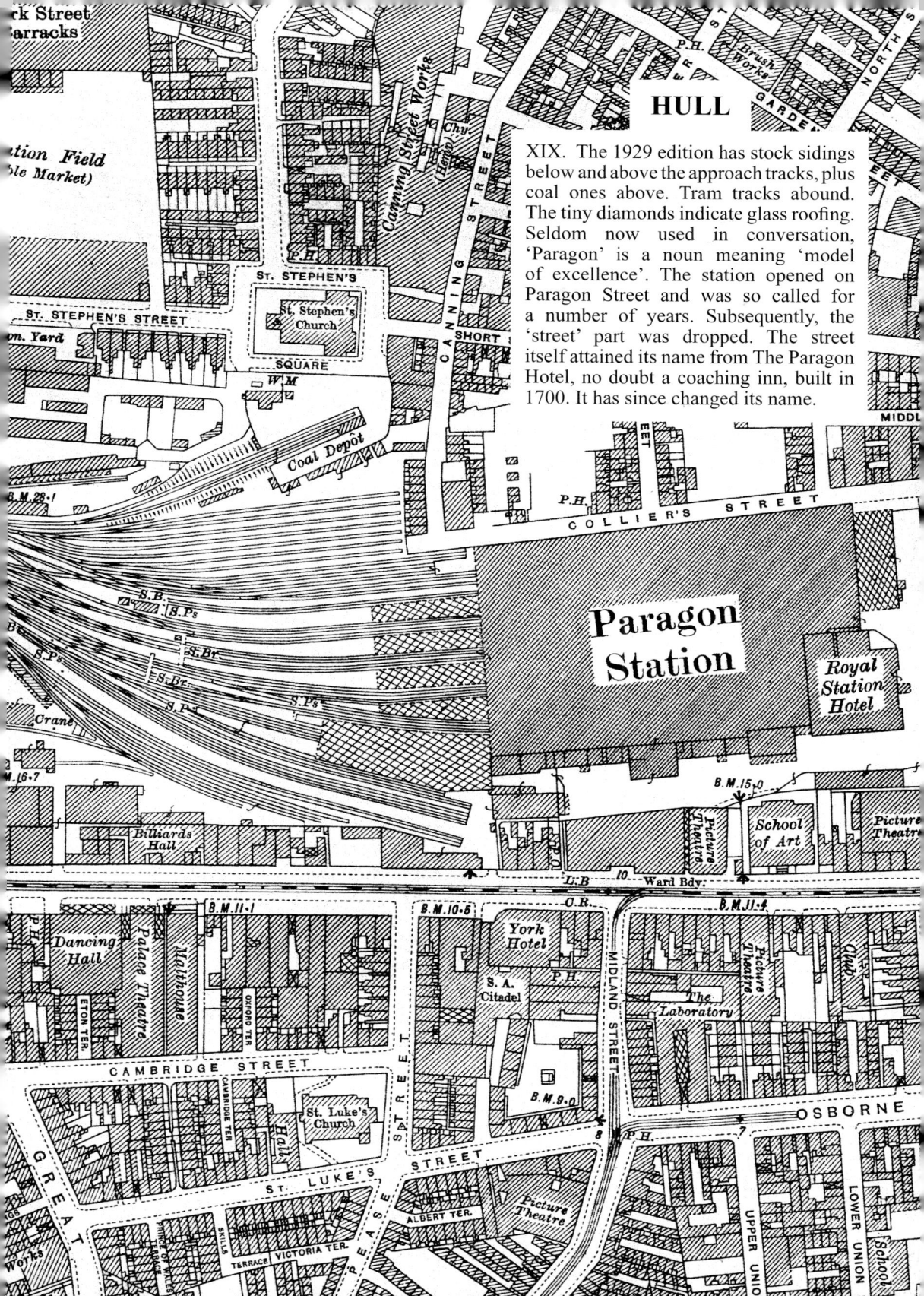

91. Parcel delivery is in progress as we enjoy the 1847 Royal Station Hotel, to be found on the right of the last map. The main station entrance is on the right of this view from around 1900. (P.Laming coll.)

ROYAL STATION HOTEL,
Under Management of North Eastern Railway Company.
RECENTLY ENLARGED AND IMPROVED.
ADJOINS PARAGON STATION. HOTEL PORTERS MEET TRAINS. HULL.
Most convenient and comfortable for Families and Gentlemen.
Telegrams: "NEROTEL, HULL." National Tel. No. 128. Corporation Telephones Nos. 134 & 135.
New Grill Room and Up-to-Date Tea Room on the Platform.
Passengers travelling on the North Eastern Railway System can Telegraph, free of charge, to secure Rooms on applying to the Company's Station Master at any Telegraph Station.

N.E.R. HOTELS

THE VITTORIA HOTEL, HULL.
FIRST-CLASS FAMILY AND COMMERCIAL.
Unrivalled situation. Facing the Humber and New Corporation Pier, one minute from Great Central Landing Stage.
Good Billiard and Smoking Rooms.
Proprietress, Mrs. ATWOOD.

BRADSHAW'S CONTINENTAL PHRASE BOOKS.
FRENCH, GERMAN, ITALIAN, OR SPANISH.
Price, One Shilling Each.
BRADSHAW HOUSE, Surrey Street, Strand, London, W.C.

Bradshaw, July 1910.

92. We are inside to enjoy the concourse and the curves of the glazed roofing. Initially the Y&NMR leased areas of the terminus to the H&SR. Trains from the east also used it from the 1860s. A bus station arrived on the north side in the mid-1930s. (J.Alsop coll.)

Excerpt from *Bradshaw's Descriptive Hand Book*, 1866.

HULL (Kingston-upon-Hull).

Telegraph stations at Nos. 37, 52, and 53, Lowgate, 6, Minerva Place, Quay Side, and Railway stations.

HOTELS.—Royal Station Hotel, for families, private or commercial gentlemen ; The George ; Glover's Commercial Hotel ; Vittoria Hotel on the Quay.

POST HORSES, FLYS, &c., at the hotels. Tariff— 1s. 6d. per mile. 1s. from any railway station to the town.

MARKET DAYS—Tuesday and Friday.

PLACES OF RESORT, &c., IN HULL.

The BOTANICAL GARDENS are on the Anlaby Road. An agreeable resort to the pleasure-seeker and practical botanist. Admission by order from subscribers.

QUEEN'S THEATRE, Paragon Street.

The LITERARY and PHILOSOPHICAL SOCIETY'S MUSEUM—ROYAL INSTITUTION, Albion Street. Admission by orders from any of the directors or subscribers.

The MUSEUM of the MECHANICS' INSTITUTE may be viewed on application to the Librarian at the Institute, George Street.

Mr. SEAMEN'S MUSUEM is at that gentleman's residence, near the Cemetery, and contains many valuable natural curiosities.

MISCELLANEOUS SOCIETIES.—Amongst the societies designed to improve the social condition of the people, may be noticed the Hull Temperance League ; the Hull Auxiliary Peace Society, W. Morley, Esq., President ; and the Vocal Society— Conductor, Mr Skelton.

This parliamentary borough and old town, founded by Edward I., as a King's Town, or Kingston-upon-Hull (which is still its official name), stands on the *Yorkshire* side of the Humber, in a very flat and uninviting spot, but admirably fitted for trade, which has much augmented in the last few years. Population, 97,661, who send two members. The river Humber, the main estuary into which the Ouse and the Yorkshire streams, with the Trent, all four flow, is here 2 miles broad, and widens to 5 or 6 before it joins the sea at Spurn Head, which is 20 miles below. All this coast of the East Riding is in progress of change—the sea gaining on the shores of the north sea, where Ravenspur, Potterfleet, and other ports, once in existence, have been swallowed up, while it is retiring, if anything, on the Hull shore, where Sunk Island (towards Spurn Head), which first appeared above water in 1630, is now a fertile cultivated tract of 4,500 acres in extent. So flat is the country that the railway to Selby westward, though 31 miles long, runs for the most part on a made embankment, and has neither tunnel nor viaduct. The loss of the ancient sea ports of the Riding led to the foundation of Hull.

Brick clay is abundant, and Hull has several specimens of *very old* brick buildings. The *Citadel* with its old moated fortress contained the barracks and magazines, and stood two sieges in the civil war ; the first being in 1642, when the refusal of Sir J. Hotham, the Governor, to deliver the town to Charles I., who appeared in person before it, was the first act of hostility between the King and Parliament. Hotham in the next year proving treacherous, was executed at Tower Hill. A bridge of three arches crosses the Hull in the middle of the town, near the upper entrance of the *Docks*, which form a loop with it and the Humber, and contain 30 acres, besides two basins of 3 acres more. *Queen's Dock*, cut in 1778, contains 13 acres, and is 1,700 feet by 254 feet ; the others are the *Humber's Prince, Railway*, and *Victoria Docks*, and all surrounded by large warehouses, and timber yards.

93. The 12.05 to Doncaster is departing on 10th May 1946 hauled by class D11 4-4-0 no. 5502 *Zeebrugge*, showing the wartime abbreviated letters on its tender. The white windows are to hide toilet compartments. Clear windows labelled 'Ladies Only' were finally discontinued in 1977, the last being on some Liverpool Street services. (H.C.Casserley)

94. The entrance glimpsed in picture 91 becomes clearer and it is now apparent that you could climb down from your horse and carriage in the dry. It is 1957 and some motor cars still had separate wings to keep their bodies clean. The fine canopy was replaced by an office block for BR in 1962. (R.Humm coll.)

95. We move forward to 26th July 1980 and witness DMU no. 51966 departing for Manchester. The massive train shed had been completed in 1904, but it was largely destroyed by bombs on 7th May 1941. Resignalling had taken place in 1935, using all electrical systems. Many platforms were renumbered in 1984. (T.Heavyside)

96. It is 18th July 2013 and the 15.10 leaves for Kings Cross. The new Hull Trains operated a weekday service of 7 trains in each direction to London. At weekends this service was reduced, with 6 trains on Saturday and 5 on Sunday. Every day one train to London started at Beverley, progressing onto Hull in the early morning, with one late night train from London terminating at Beverley. (J.Whitehouse)

97. The word 'Interchange' appears in this view from 8th May 2017. This creation opened on 16th September 2007, combining rail and bus station services on a single site. The bus terminal has 38 bus and four coach stands, replacing a separate 'island' bus station. The site of the former Hull Bus Station, adjacent to the north of the railway station, now forms part of the St. Stephen's shopping centre. (Colour-Rail.com)

98. On the left is DMU no. 185112 of TransPennine Express waiting to depart at 11.40 to Manchester on 7th June 2018. This company managed the entire station at that time. The station is listed Grade II. (R.J.Stewart-Smith)

2. Gilberdyke to Selby
EASTRINGTON

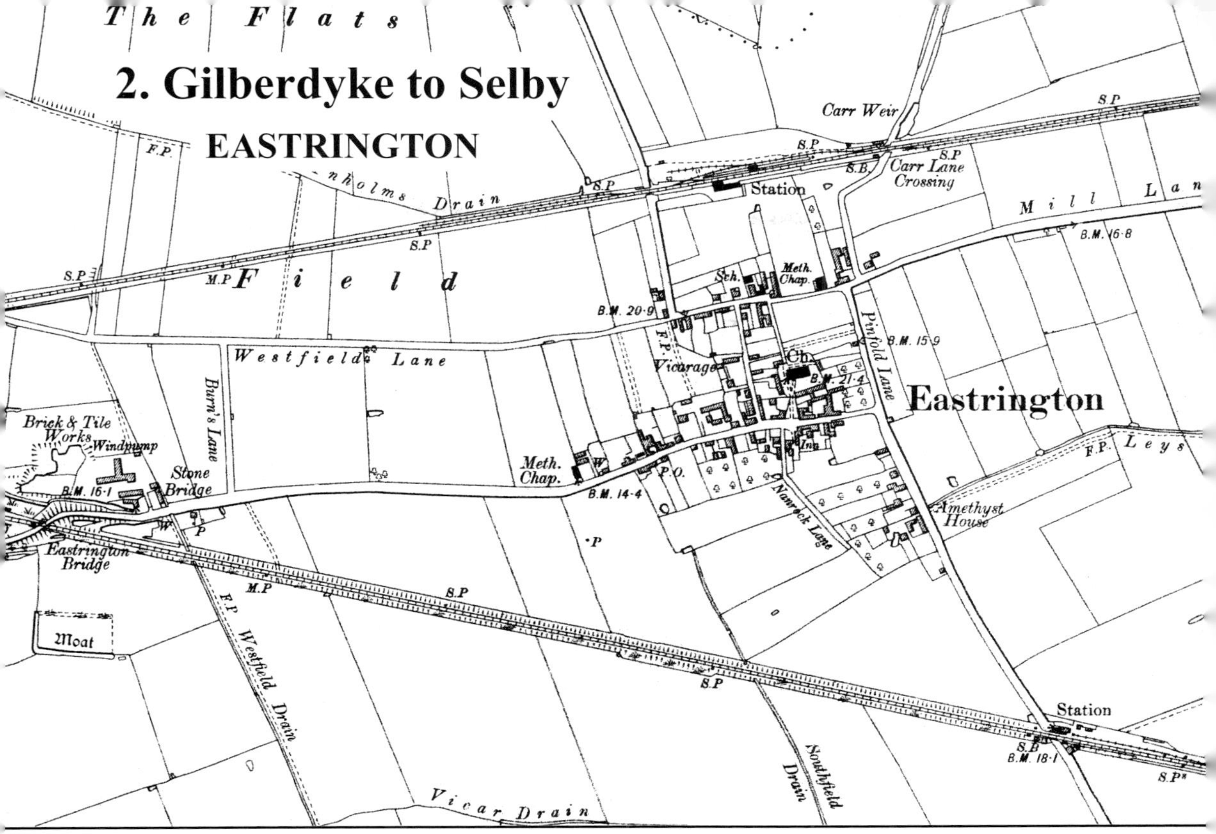

XX. If we return to map II, top centre, we find Eastrington, plus the straight route west to Selby, top left. This 1920 issue at 6ins to 1 mile has this station lower right, with one siding. North station is near the top and was served by trains on the Hull and Barnsley line, from 1885 to 1959.

99. The village housed 421 folk in 1921 and is shown to have a church and a chapel, plus Vicar Drain. The prefix SOUTH was used from 1st July 1922 until 12th June 1961. Beyond the van are a loading gauge and a locomotive shunting. (P.Laming coll.)

100. Sleepers are being replaced in about 1939. One chimney pot has a smoke hood, not an intruding bird. The goods yard was closed on 4th May 1964. There was a 15-lever signal box nearby at Caville Bridge until 1938. (Stations UK)

101. The old waiting room was in poor condition on 21st June 1986, but the two staff cottages and the signal appeared to be in good form. The box was opened by 1905, with 25 levers, and closed on 17th September 1989. (R.J.Stewart-Smith)

102. It is 2nd April 2001 and Northern Spirit DMU no. 156497 passes with the 12.56 Manchester Airport–Hull. The station stands quietly in open countryside, a few minutes walk from the village along the lane to the right. Simple shelters of different designs provide the passenger facilities. By 2015, the annual passengers numbered 1282. (A.C.Hartless)

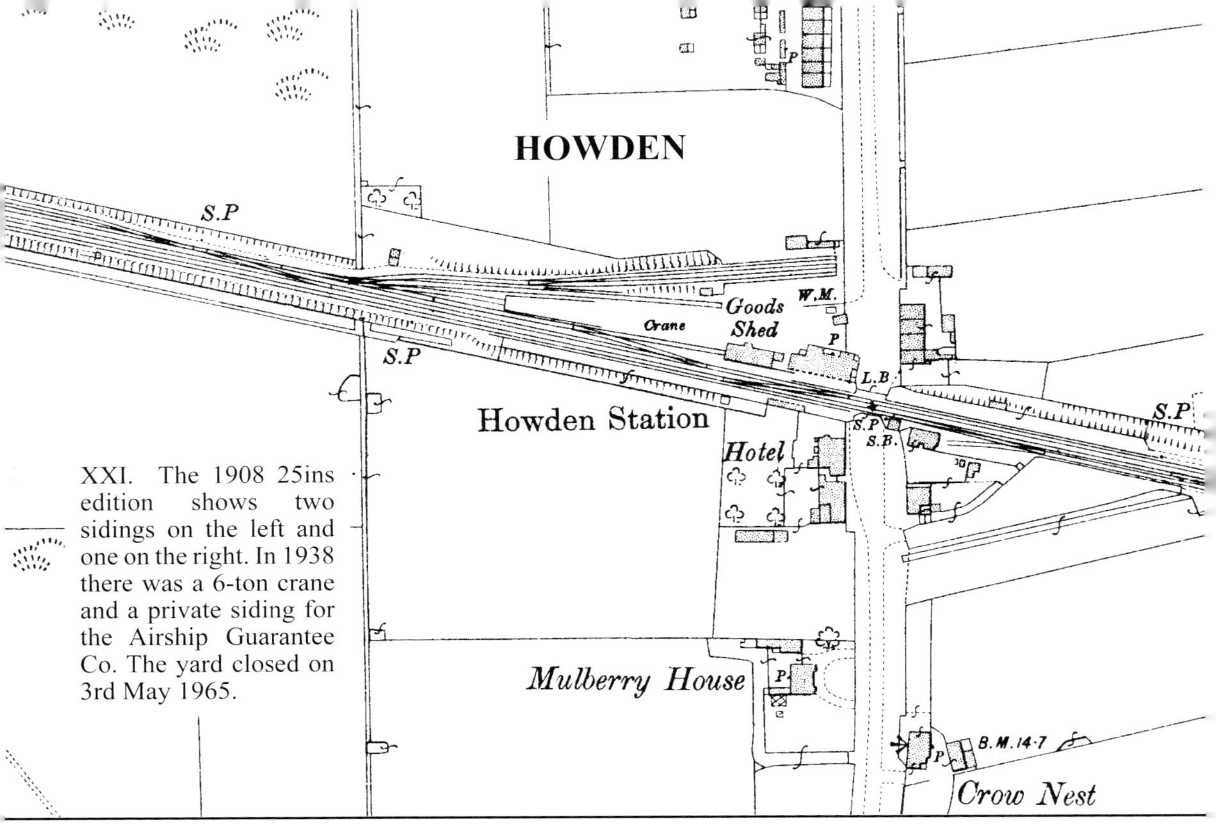
HOWDEN
S.P
Crane
Goods Shed
W.M.
P
L.B.
S.P
Howden Station
S.B.
Hotel
Mulberry House
B.M. 14·7
Crow Nest

XXI. The 1908 25ins edition shows two sidings on the left and one on the right. In 1938 there was a 6-ton crane and a private siding for the Airship Guarantee Co. The yard closed on 3rd May 1965.

103. It is 30th March 2015 and TransPennine Express unit no. 185149 runs past with the 08.41 Manchester Piccadilly–Hull. The derelict signal box no longer controls the level crossing over the B1228, which a truck is waiting to cross. The down platform, on which the photographer stands, was originally on the other side of the road. Residents numbered 1986 in 1901 and 2282 in 1961. The box opened in about 1873 and had 31 levers from 1905, for a period. Closure came on 8th November 1997. (A.C.Hartless)

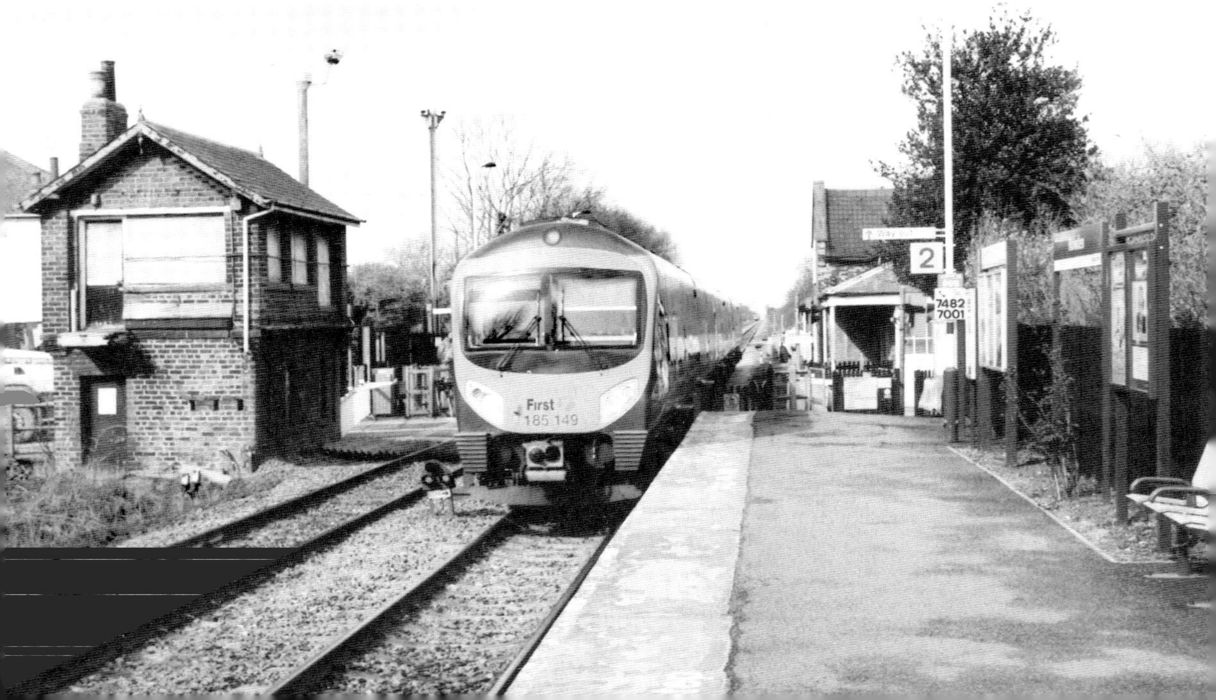
First
185 149
2

104. It is now 18th July 2013 and anti-trespasser bars isolate them from the remotely controlled reversing point. The dwelling for the station master had long been in private ownership, by that time. (J.Whitehouse)

105. A panorama from 9th June 2020 records the staggering of the platforms. This system was used to make alighting passengers cross the tracks behind departing trains. Lengthy lifting barriers adorn the scene. (A.J.Booth)

WRESSLE

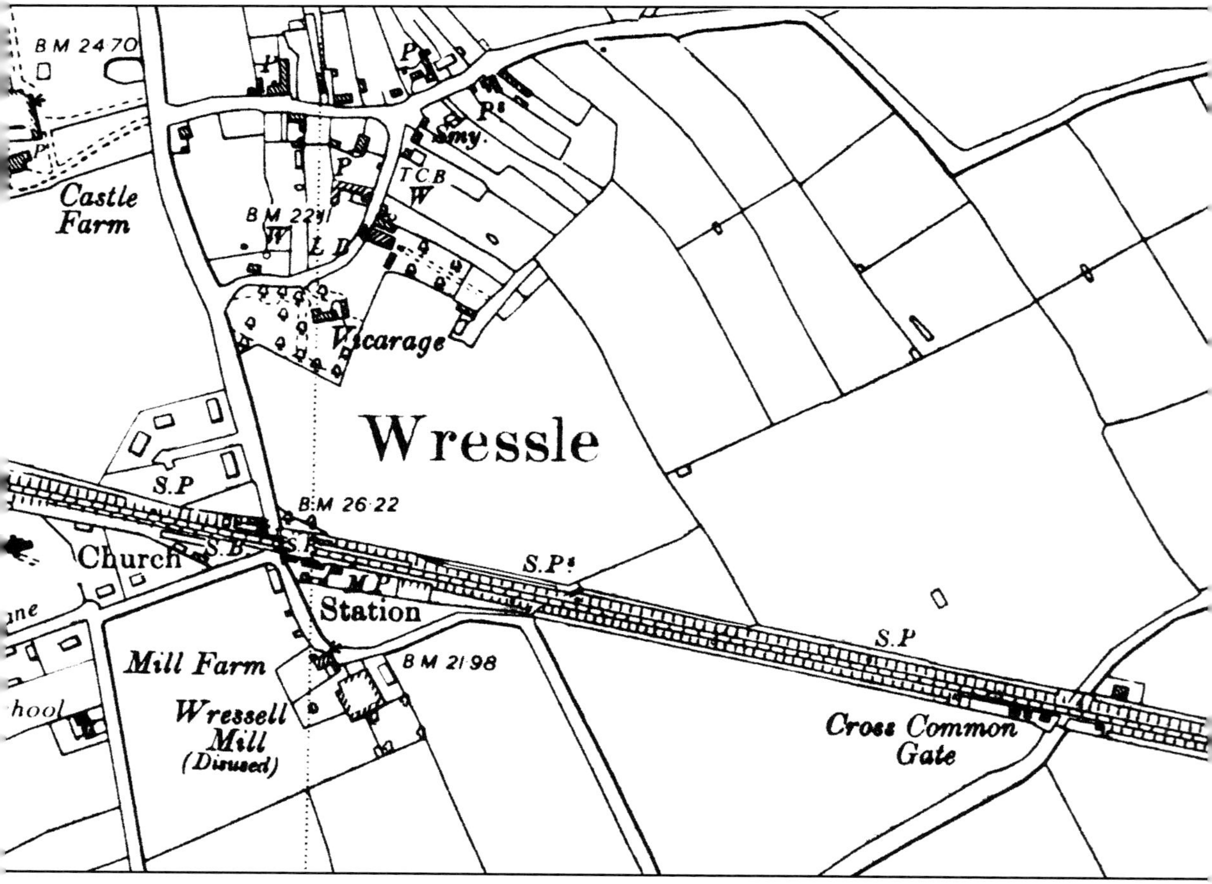

XXII. The 1950 issue at about 8ins to 1 mile includes an alternative spelling, on the mill, one of several used in the early days. The service then varied; it was market days only for many years. By 1901, the population had grown to 275. The village is close by and still has a smithy, marked as 'Smy'.

106. This view from 19th July 1958 has both platforms beyond the gates. The goods yard was in use until 4th May 1964 and the signalman appears to be retiring. When his box closed on 13th July 1986, it only had 10 of its 21 levers left. (R.Humm coll.)

107. Looking in the other direction on 9th June 2020, we see unit nos 185108 and 185113. It seems that the flat bottom track is having to be replaced in parts. (A.J.Booth)

HEMINGBROUGH

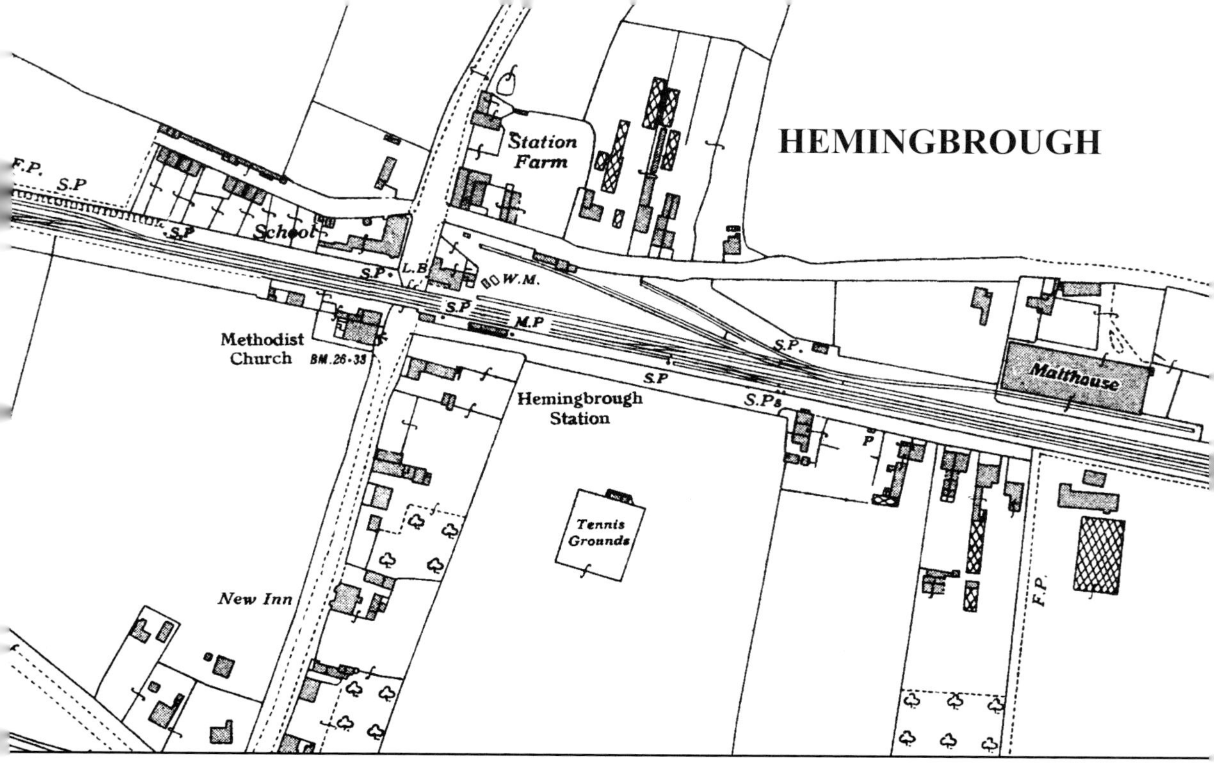

XXIII. The 1938 data at about 20ins to 1 mile includes a private siding for J.Smith's Tadcaster Brewery. The station was built within the village of Cliffe, over one mile from Hemingbrough. The latter's population rose from 498 in 1901 to 693 in 1961.

108. We look west on 2nd March 1957 as the 3.30pm Leeds to Hull runs in behind class B1 4-6-0 no. 61237 *Geoffrey H.Kitson*. Passenger service ceased here on 6th November 1967. (R.Humm coll.)

109. No. 61256 of the same class, but devoid of a name, is on the crossing. We are in the goods yard, which was closed on 4th May 1964. The hut on the right housed the office for the weighing machine. The tallest building on the left was the Methodist Chapel. (Book Law)

110. This record dates from 6th July 1986 and features the box, which once had a 32-lever frame. It was replaced by a 22-lever version in 1968 and was closed on 3rd November 1997. The barriers became automatic. (R.J.Stewart-Smith)

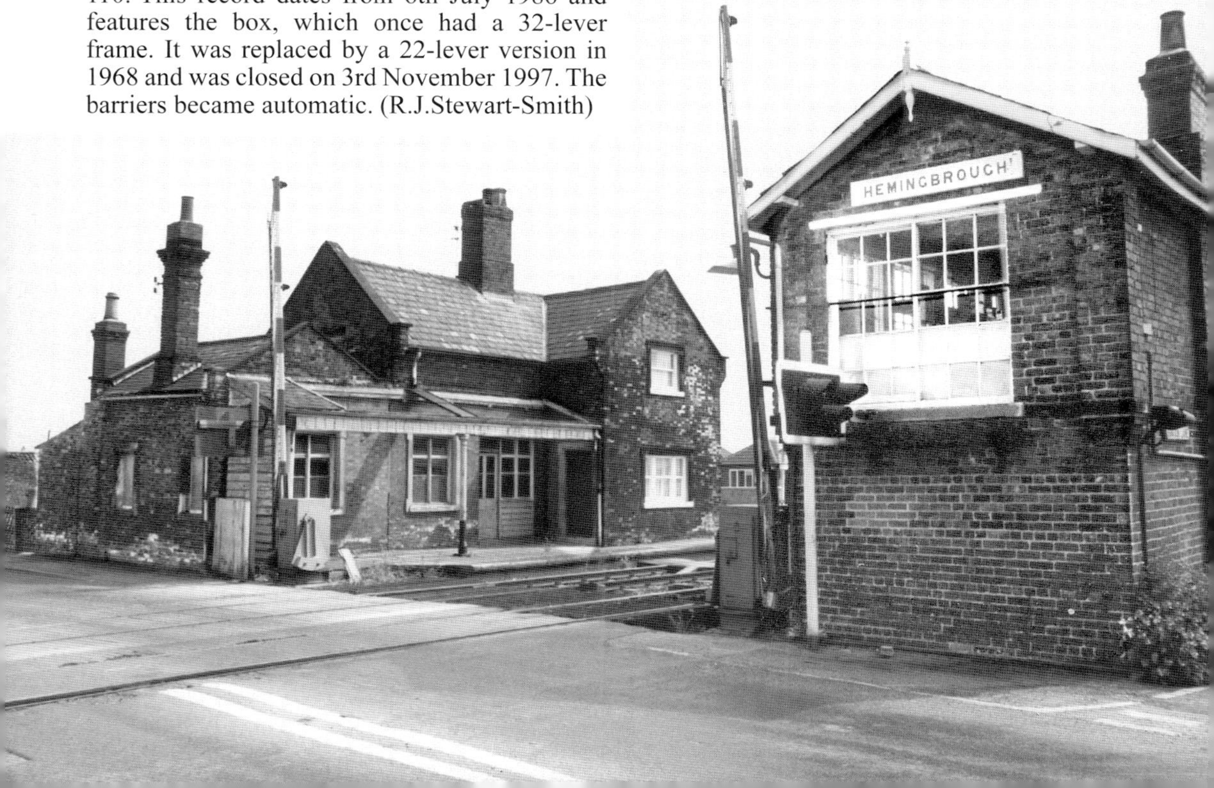

EAST OF SELBY

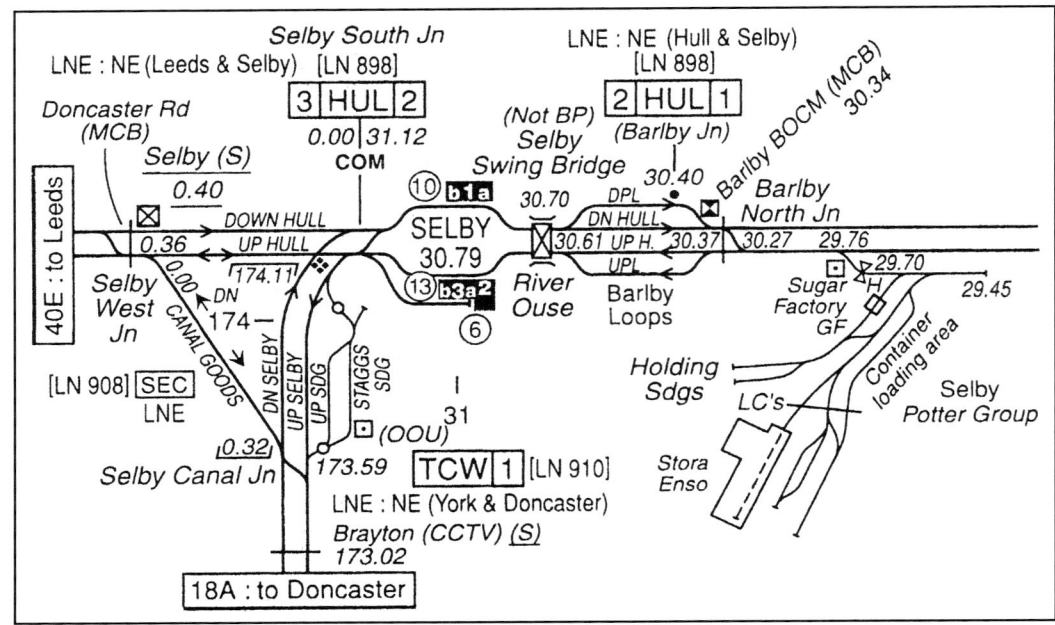

XXIV. We arrive on the right of this 2016 diagram. BOCM refers to the British Oil & Cake Mills animal feed manufacturer, and MCB to a manually-controlled barrier. (©TRACKmaps)

111. Barlby North box and the extensive yard were recorded in about 1960. The former opened on 27th November 1898 with two large lever frames. The yard was eventually reduced to two passing loops. The box was closed on 23rd January 1972. (R.Humm coll.)

112. Barlby signal box is seen in 1958 with the BOCM animal feed factory behind. The latter has since been demolished. Two shunting signals are evident, on short posts. The signal box was in use from 1898 until 23rd January 1972. (R.Humm coll.)

XXV. The 1950 edition at about 4ins to 1 mile has the station lower left and our arrival line on the right, the lower one. 'BSW↑D' indicates 'Boundary Stone War Department'. Selby Coalfield was beyond the left border and was worked from the early 1980s to November 2004. Cliff signal box is on the right.

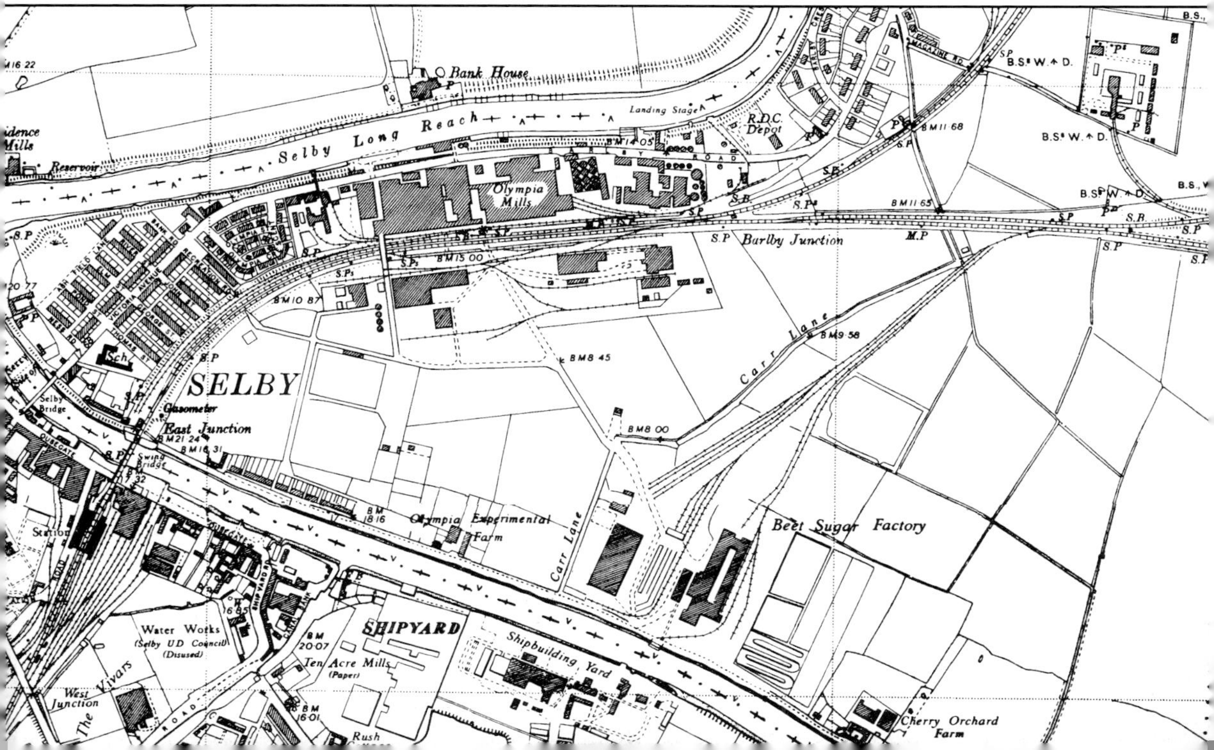

113. John Fowler of Leeds built this 0-4-0 diesel mechanical loco, which was fitted with a 150hp engine. It was works no. 4200003, which was ex-works on 23rd March 1946 to BOCM, Stoneferry Works, Hull, and later transferred to their Selby site, where it is seen on 26th August 1978. (A.J.Booth)

114. The Potter Group established a successful freight railhead on the former British Sugar site on the east side of Selby. Sentinel 0-6-0 locomotive with maker's no. 10220 waits in the unloading shed on 13th June 2002. At that time, the terminal received a daily trainload of paper from Felixstowe, a daily trainload of paper from Immingham, a three times weekly GB Railfreight intermodal service from Felixstowe, a twice weekly stone train from Peak Forest and a daily Enterprise wagonload service from Doncaster. (P.D.Shannon)

115. This overview of the Potter Group terminal on 15th July 2008 shows the stone discharge facility on the right and the container handling area on the left. No. 66168 is about to depart after calling at the terminal with the 17.56 Enterprise wagonload train from Immingham to Mossend. (P.D.Shannon)

116. We are approaching Selby Swing Bridge from the east on 27th September 1963, with the control cabin prominent. This was the joint SLS/RCTS North Eastern Rail Tour. It is approaching the 1891 replacement bridge, which was refurbished in 2014, to give modern controls. The station is beyond. In 1960, the cabin had been raised 3ft 6ins permanently, over two weekends. (H.C.Casserley)

SELBY

117. Selby North and the Swing Bridge boxes are both visible as an express arrives, bound for Kings Cross some time in the 1950s. No. 60129 *Guy Mannering* is a class A1 4-6-2, a successful type which started production in 1948. (R.S.Carpenter coll.)

118. The 09.45 Yarmouth to Newcastle runs in on 9th August 1976, hauled by no. 40051. Many class 47 Co-Cos undertook freight work, as well. (T.Heavyside)

119. Seen on 2nd November 1987 is the west end of the two through platforms, with all the fine details of the original (dating from 2nd July 1840). Until then, there was just a terminal building, the end of which was close to the River Ouse. It had received trains from Leeds since 22nd September 1834 and is the tallest building on the left of picture 116. (D.A.Thompson/Middleton Press coll.)

The many changes that have taken place west of the station, and near the colliery, can be found in captions 68-70 in *Leeds to Selby and Goole*.

120. We have a final peep at the swing bridge as Arriva Trains Northern unit no. 158776 comes to a stand on 16th March 2003. Many visitors now rest here to enjoy the central garden shrubs. The Selby Diversion of 1983 for north-south main line trains had made the centre tracks obsolete. (M.P.Turvey)

EVOLVING THE

ULTIMATE RAIL ENCYCLOPEDIA

INTERNATIONAL

Easebourne Midhurst GU29 9AZ. Tel:01730 813169

A-978 0 906520 B- 978 1 873793 C- 978 1 901706 D-978 1 904474 E - 978 1 906008 F - 978 1 908174 G - 978 1 910356

Our RAILWAY titles are listed below. Please check availability by looking at our website www.middletonpress.co.uk, telephoning us or by requesting a Brochure which includes our LATEST RAILWAY TITLES also our TRAMWAY, TROLLEYBUS, MILITARY and COASTAL series.

email:info@middletonpress.co.uk

A

Abergavenny to Merthyr C 91 8
Abertillery & Ebbw Vale Lines D 84 5
Aberystwyth to Carmarthen E 90 1
Allhallows - Branch Line to A 62 8
Alton - Branch Lines to A 11 6
Ambergate to Buxton G 28 9
Ambergate to Mansfield G 39 5
Andover to Southampton A 82 6
Ascot - Branch Lines around A 64 2
Ashburton - Branch Line to B 95 4
Ashford - Steam to Eurostar B 67 1
Ashford to Dover A 48 2
Austrian Narrow Gauge D 04 3
Avonmouth - BL around D 42 5
Aylesbury to Rugby D 91 3

B

Baker Street to Uxbridge D 90 6
Bala to Llandudno E 87 1
Banbury to Birmingham D 27 2
Banbury to Cheltenham E 63 5
Bangor to Holyhead F 01 7
Bangor to Portmadoc E 72 7
Barking to Southend C 80 2
Barmouth to Pwllheli E 53 6
Barry - Branch Lines around D 50 0
Bartlow - Branch Lines to F 27 7
Basingstoke to Salisbury A 89 4
Bath Green Park to Bristol C 36 9
Bath to Evercreech Junction A 60 4
Beamish 40 years on rails E94 9
Bedford to Wellingborough D 31 9
Berwick to Drem F 64 2
Berwick to St. Boswells F 75 8
B'ham to Tamworth & Nuneaton F 63 5
Birkenhead to West Kirby F 61 1
Birmingham to Wolverhampton E253
Blackburn to Hellifield F 95 6
Bletchley to Cambridge D 94 4
Bletchley to Rugby E 07 9
Bodmin - Branch Lines around B 83 1
Boston to Lincoln F 80 2
Bournemouth to Evercreech Jn A 46 8
Bournemouth to Weymouth A 57 4
Bradshaw's History F18 5
Bradshaw's Rail Times 1850 F 13 0
Branch Lines series - see town names
Brecon to Neath D 43 2
Brecon to Newport D 16 6
Brecon to Newtown E 06 2
Brighton to Eastbourne A 16 1
Brighton to Worthing A 03 1
Bristol to Taunton D 03 6
Bromley South to Rochester B 23 7
Bromsgrove to Birmingham D 87 6
Bromsgrove to Gloucester D 73 9
Broxbourne to Cambridge F16 1
Brunel - A railtour D 74 6
Bude - Branch Line to B 29 9
Burnham to Evercreech Jn B 68 0
Buxton to Stockport G 32 6

C

Cambridge to Ely D 55 5
Canterbury - BLs around B 58 9
Cardiff to Dowlais (Cae Harris) E 47 5
Cardiff to Pontypridd E 95 6
Cardiff to Swansea E 42 0
Carlisle to Hawick E 85 7
Carmarthen to Fishguard E 66 6
Caterham & Tattenham Corner B251
Central & Southern Spain NG E 91 8
Chard and Yeovil - BLs a C 30 7
Charing Cross to Dartford A 75 8
Charing Cross to Orpington A 96 3
Cheddar - Branch Line to B 90 9
Cheltenham to Andover C 43 7
Cheltenham to Redditch D 81 4
Chester to Birkenhead F 21 5
Chester to Manchester F 51 2
Chester to Rhyl E 93 2
Chester to Warrington F 40 6
Chesterfield to Lincoln G 21 0
Chesterfield to Rotherham G 48 7
Chichester to Portsmouth A 14 7
Clacton and Walton - BLs to F 04 8
Clapham Jn to Beckenham Jn B 36 7
Cleobury Mortimer - BLs a E 18 5
Clevedon & Portishead - BLs to D180
Consett to South Shields E 57 4
Cornwall Narrow Gauge D 56 2
Corris and Vale of Rheidol E 65 9
Coventry to Leicester G 00 5
Craven Arms to Llandeilo E 35 2
Craven Arms to Wellington E 33 8
Crawley to Littlehampton A 34 5
Crewe to Manchester F 57 4
Crewe to Wigan G 12 8
Cromer - Branch Lines around C 26 0
Cromford and High Peak G 35 7
Croydon to East Grinstead B 48 0
Crystal Palace & Catford Loop B 87 1
Cyprus Narrow Gauge E 13 0

D

Darjeeling Revisited F 09 3
Darlington Leamside Newcastle E 28 4
Darlington to Newcastle D 98 2
Dartford to Sittingbourne B 34 3
Denbigh - Branch Lines around F 32 1
Derby to Chesterfield G 11 1
Derby to Nottingham G 45 6
Derby to Stoke-on-Trent F 93 2
Derwent Valley - BL to the D 06 7
Devon Narrow Gauge E 09 3
Didcot to Banbury D 02 9
Didcot to Swindon C 84 0
Didcot to Winchester C 13 0
Diss to Norwich G 22 7
Doncaster to Hull G 49 4
Dorset & Somerset NG D 76 0
Douglas - Laxey - Ramsey E 75 8
Douglas to Peel C 88 8
Douglas to Port Erin C 55 0
Douglas to Ramsey D 39 5
Dover to Ramsgate A 78 9
Drem to Edinburgh G 06 7
Dublin Northwards in 1950s E 31 4
Dunstable - Branch Lines to E 27 7

E

Ealing to Slough C 42 0
Eastbourne to Hastings A 27 7
East Cornwall Mineral Railways D 22 7
East Croydon to Three Bridges A 53 6
Eastern Spain Narrow Gauge E 56 7
East Grinstead - BLs to A 07 9
East Kent Light Railway A 61 1
East London - Branch Lines of C 44 4
East London Line B 80 0
East of Norwich - Branch Lines E 69 7
Effingham Junction - BLs a A 74 1
Ely to Norwich C 90 1
Enfield Town & Palace Gates D 32 6
Epsom to Horsham A 30 7
Eritrean Narrow Gauge E 38 3
Euston to Harrow & Wealdstone C 89 5
Exeter to Barnstaple B 15 2
Exeter to Newton Abbot C 49 9
Exeter to Tavistock B 69 5
Exmouth - Branch Lines to B 00 8

F

Fairford - Branch Line to A 52 9
Falmouth, Helston & St. Ives C 74 1
Fareham to Salisbury A 67 3
Faversham to Dover B 05 3
Felixstowe & Aldeburgh - BL to D 20 3
Fenchurch Street to Barking C 20 8
Festiniog - 50 yrs of enterprise C 83 3
Festiniog 1946-55 E 01 7
Festiniog in the Fifties B 68 8
Festiniog in the Sixties B 91 6
Ffestiniog in Colour 1955-82 F 25 3
Finsbury Park to Alexandra Pal C 02 8
French Metre Gauge Survivors F 88 8
Frome to Bristol B 77 0

G

Gainsborough to Sheffield G 17 3
Galashiels to Edinburgh F 52 9
Gloucester to Bristol D 35 7
Gloucester to Cardiff D 66 1
Gosport - Branch Lines around A 36 9
Greece Narrow Gauge D 72 2
Guildford to Redhill A 63 5

H

Hampshire Narrow Gauge D 36 4
Harrow to Watford D 14 2
Harwich & Hadleigh - BLs to F 02 4
Harz Revisited F 62 8
Hastings to Ashford A 37 6
Hawick to Galashiels F 36 9
Hawkhurst - Branch Line to A 66 6
Hayling - Branch Line to A 12 3
Hay-on-Wye - BL around D 92 0
Haywards Heath to Seaford A 28 4
Hemel Hempstead - BLs to D 88 3
Henley, Windsor & Marlow - BLa C77 2
Hereford to Newport D 54 8
Hertford & Hatfield - BLs a E 58 1
Hertford Loop E 71 0
Hexham to Carlisle D 75 3
Hexham to Hawick F 08 6
Hitchin to Peterborough D 07 4
Holborn Viaduct to Lewisham A 81 9
Horsham - Branch Lines to A 02 4
Hull, Hornsea and Withernsea G 27 2
Huntingdon - Branch Line to A 93 2

I

Ilford to Shenfield C 97 0
Ilfracombe - Branch Line to B 21 3
Ilkeston to Chesterfield G 26 5
Ipswich to Diss F 81 9
Ipswich to Saxmundham C 41 3
Isle of Man Railway Journey F 94 9
Isle of Wight Lines - 50 yrs C 12 3
Italy Narrow Gauge F 17 8

K

Kent Narrow Gauge C 45 1
Kettering to Nottingham F 82-6
Kidderminster to Shrewsbury E 10 9
Kingsbridge - Branch Line to C 98 7
Kings Cross to Potters Bar E 62 8
King's Lynn to Hunstanton F 58 1
Kingston & Hounslow Loops A 83 3
Kingswear - Branch Line to C 17 8

L

Lambourn - Branch Line to C 70 3
Launceston & Princetown - BLs C 19 2
Leeds to Selby and Goole G 47 0
Leek - Branch Line From G 01 2
Leicester to Burton F 85 7
Leicester to Nottingham G 15 9
Lewisham to Dartford A 92 5
Lincoln to Cleethorpes F 56 7
Lincoln to Doncaster G 03 6
Lines around Stamford F 98 7
Lines around Wimbledon B 75 6
Lines North of Stoke G 29 6
Liverpool Street to Chingford D 01 2
Liverpool Street to Ilford C 34 5
Llandeilo to Swansea E 46 8
London Bridge to Addiscombe B 20 6
London Bridge to East Croydon A 58 1
Longmoor - Branch Lines to A 41 3
Looe - Branch Line to C 22 2
Loughborough to Ilkeston G 24 1
Loughborough to Nottingham F 68 0
Lowestoft - BLs around E 40 6
Ludlow to Hereford E 14 7
Lydney - Branch Lines around E 26 0
Lyme Regis - Branch Line to A 45 1
Lynton - Branch Line to B 04 6

M

Machynlleth to Barmouth E 54 3
Maesteg and Tondu Lines F 06 2
Majorca & Corsica Narrow Gauge F 41 3
Manchester to Bacup G 46 3
Mansfield to Doncaster G 23 4
March - Branch Lines around B 09 1
Market Drayton - BLs around F 67 3
Market Harborough to Newark F 86 4
Marylebone to Rickmansworth D 49 4
Melton Constable to Yarmouth Bch E031
Midhurst - Branch Lines of E 78 9
Midhurst - Branch Lines to F 00 0
Minehead - Branch Line to A 80 2
Mitcham Junction Lines B 01 5
Monmouth - Branch Lines to E 20 8
Monmouthshire Eastern Valleys D 71 5
Moretonhampstead - BL to C 27 7
Moreton-in-Marsh to Worcester D 26 5
Morpeth to Bellingham F 87 1
Mountain Ash to Neath D 80 7

N

Newark to Doncaster F 78 9
Newbury to Westbury C 66 6
Newcastle to Alnmouth G 36 4
Newcastle to Hexham D 69 2
New Mills to Sheffield G 44 9
Newport (IOW) - Branch Lines to A 26 0
Newquay - Branch Lines to C 71 0
Newton Abbot to Plymouth C 60 4
Newtown to Aberystwyth E 41 3
Northampton to Peterborough F 92 5
North East German NG D 44 9
Northern Alpine Narrow Gauge F 37 6
Northern France Narrow Gauge C 75 8
Northern Spain Narrow Gauge E 83 3
North London Line B 94 7
North of Birmingham F 55 0
North of Grimsby - Branch Lines G 09 8
North Woolwich - BLs around C 65 9
Nottingham to Boston F 70 3
Nottingham to Kirkby Bentinck G 38 8
Nottingham to Lincoln F 43 7
Nuneaton to Loughborough G 08 1

O

Ongar - Branch Line to E 05 5
Orpington to Tonbridge B 03 9
Oswestry - Branch Lines around E 60 4
Oswestry to Whitchurch E 81 9
Oxford to Bletchley D 57 9
Oxford to Moreton-in-Marsh D 15 9

P

Paddington to Ealing C 37 6
Paddington to Princes Risborough C819
Padstow - Branch Line to B 54 1
Peebles Loop G 19 7
Pembroke and Cardigan - BLs to F 29 1
Peterborough to Kings Lynn E 32 1
Peterborough to Lincoln F 89 5
Peterborough to Newark F 72 7
Plymouth - BLs around B 98 5
Plymouth to St. Austell C 63 5
Pontypool to Mountain Ash D 65 4
Pontypridd to Merthyr F 14 7
Pontypridd to Port Talbot E 86 4
Porthmadog 1954-94 - BLa B 31 2
Portmadoc 1923-46 - BLa B 13 8
Portsmouth to Southampton A 31 4
Portugal Narrow Gauge E 67 3
Potters Bar to Cambridge D 70 8
Preston to Blackpool G 16 6
Princes Risborough - BL to D 05 0
Princes Risborough to Banbury C 85 7

R

Railways to Victory C 16 1
Reading to Basingstoke B 27 5
Reading to Didcot C 79 6
Reading to Guildford A 47 5
Redhill to Ashford A 73 4
Return to Blaenau 1970-82 C 64 2
Rhyl to Bangor F 15 4
Rhymney & New Tredegar Lines E 48 2
Rickmansworth to Aylesbury D 61 6
Romania & Bulgaria NG E 23 9
Romneyrail C 32 1
Ross-on-Wye - BLs around E 30 7
Ruabon to Barmouth E 84 0
Rugby to Birmingham E 37 6
Rugby to Loughborough F 12 3
Rugby to Stafford F 07 9
Rugeley to Stoke-on-Trent F 90 1
Ryde to Ventnor A 19 2

S

Salisbury to Westbury B 39 8
Salisbury to Yeovil B 06 0
Sardinia and Sicily Narrow Gauge F 50 5
Saxmundham to Yarmouth C 69 7
Saxony & Baltic Germany Revisited F 71 0
Saxony Narrow Gauge D 47 0
Scunthorpe to Doncaster G 34 0
Seaton & Sidmouth - BLs to A 95 6
Selsey - Branch Line to A 04 8
Sheerness - Branch Line to B 16 2
Sheffield towards Manchester G 18 0
Shenfield to Ipswich E 96 3
Shrewsbury - Branch Line to A 86 4
Shrewsbury to Chester E 70 3
Shrewsbury to Crewe F 48 2
Shrewsbury to Ludlow E 21 5
Shrewsbury to Newtown E 29 1
Sirhowy Valley Line E 12 3
Sittingbourne to Ramsgate A 90 1
Skegness & Mablethorpe - BL to F 84 0
Slough to Newbury C 56 7
South African Two-foot gauge E 51 2
Southampton to Bournemouth A 42 0
Southend & Southminster BLs E 76 5
Southern Alpine Narrow Gauge F 22 2
Southern France Narrow Gauge C 47 5
South London Line B 46 6
South Lynn to Norwich City F 03 1
Southwold - Branch Line to A 15 4
Spalding - Branch Lines around E 52 9
Spalding to Grimsby F 65 9 6
Stafford to Chester F 34 5
Stafford to Wellington F 59 8
St Albans to Bedford D 08 1
St. Austell to Penzance C 67 3
St. Boswell to Berwick F 44 4
Steaming Through Isle of Wight A 56 7
Stourbridge to Wolverhampton E 16 1
St. Pancras to Barking D 68 5
St. Pancras to Folkestone E 88 8
St. Pancras to St. Albans C 78 9
Stratford to Cheshunt F 53 6
Stratford-u-Avon to Birmingham D 77 7
Stratford-u-Avon to Cheltenham C 25 3
Sudbury - Branch Lines to F 19 2
Surrey Narrow Gauge C 87 1
Sussex Narrow Gauge C 68 0
Swaffham - Branch Lines around F 97 0
Swanage to 1999 - BL to A 33 8
Swanley to Ashford B 45 9
Swansea - Branch Lines around F 38 3
Swansea to Carmarthen E 59 8
Swindon to Bristol C 96 3
Swindon to Gloucester D 46 3
Swindon to Newport D 30 2
Swiss Narrow Gauge C 94 9

T

Talyllyn 60 E 98 7
Tamworth to Derby F 76 5
Taunton to Barnstaple B 60 2
Taunton to Exeter C 82 6
Taunton to Minehead F 39 0
Tavistock to Plymouth B 88 6
Tenterden - Branch Line to A 21 5
Three Bridges to Brighton A 35 2
Tilbury Loop C 86 4
Tiverton - BLs around C 62 8
Tivetshall to Beccles D 41 8
Tonbridge to Hastings A 44 4
Torrington - Branch Lines to B 37 4
Tourist Railways of France G 04 3
Towcester - BLs around E 39 0
Tunbridge Wells BLs A 32 1

U

Upwell - Branch Line to B 64 0
Uttoxeter to Macclesfield G 05 0
Uttoxetor to Buxton G 33 3

V

Victoria to Bromley South A 98 7
Victoria to East Croydon A 40 6
Vivarais Revisited E 08 6

W

Walsall Routes F 45 1
Wantage - Branch Line to D 25 8
Wareham to Swanage 50 yrs D 09 8
Waterloo to Windsor A 54 3
Waterloo to Woking A 38 3
Watford to Leighton Buzzard D 45 6
Wellingborough to Leicester F 73 4
Welshpool to Llanfair E 49 9
Wenford Bridge to Fowey C 09 3
Westbury to Bath B 55 8
Westbury to Taunton C 76 5
West Cornwall Mineral Rlys D 48 7
West Croydon to Epsom B 08 4
West German Narrow Gauge D 93 7
West London - BLs of C 50 5
West London Line B 84 8
West Wiltshire - BLs of D 12 8
Weymouth - BLs A 65 9
Willesden Jn to Richmond B 71 8
Wimbledon to Beckenham C 58 1
Wimbledon to Epsom B 62 6
Wimborne - BLs around A 97 0
Wirksworth - Branch Lines to G 10 4
Wisbech - BLs around C 01 7
Witham & Kelvedon - BLs a E 82 6
Woking to Alton A 59 8
Woking to Portsmouth A 25 3
Woking to Southampton A 55 0
Wolverhampton to Shrewsbury E 44 4
Wolverhampton to Stafford F 79 6
Worcester to Birmingham D 97 5
Worcester to Hereford D 38 8
Worthing to Chichester A 06 2
Wrexham to New Brighton F 47 5
Wroxham - BLs around F 31 4

Y

Yeovil - 50 yrs change C 38 3
Yeovil to Dorchester A 76 5
Yeovil to Exeter A 91 8
York to Scarborough F 23 9